FAMILY BIBLE STORY

JOSEPH

Presented to

....

by

....

on this date

....

To order, call

1-800-765-6955.

FAMILY BIBLE STORY

JOSEPH

Text by
RUTH REDDING BRAND

Color paintings by Jack Pennington

Pencil Illustrations by Darrel Tank

REVIEW AND HERALD® PUBLISHING ASSOCIATION
HAGERSTOWN, MD 21740

Scriptures credited to ICB are quoted from the *International Children's Bible, New Century Version,* copyright © 1983, 1986, 1988 by Word Publishing, Dallas, Texas 75039. Used by permission.

This book was
Edited by Richard W. Coffen
Copyedited by Jocelyn Fay and James Cavil
Designed by Trent Truman
Cover art by Jack Pennington and Darrel Tank
Typeset: Galliard 13/22

PRINTED IN U.S.A.

08 07 06 05 04   5 4 3 2 1

R&H Cataloging Service
Family Bible Story: Joseph
        V.

    1. Bible Stories. I. Brand, Ruth Redding

        220.9505

ISBN 0-8280-1854-5   hardcover
ISBN 0-8280-1855-3   paperback

DEDICATED TO

Gail Hunt—

artist, designer, musician,
dreamer, genius, and

the inspiration for this book.

CONTENTS

HOW TO USE THIS BOOK

This book looks interesting, with its various parts, but it also looks rather confusing. How does one make sense of the several elements throughout? How, exactly, does one use this book?

Perhaps it might help if we unpack the name Family Bible Story.

The last two words, "Bible Story," explain what the book is really all about—Bible stories. Within these covers you'll find material that makes Bible stories come alive for contemporary readers.

We live in an age of burgeoning biblical ignorance. Even people who call themselves Christians remain unfamiliar with the content, even the stories, found in the Judeo-Christian Scriptures.

"Increasingly, America is biblically illiterate," pollster George Barna has said, and he had evidence to support such a claim. His studies revealed that 60 percent of Americans cannot name half of the Ten Commandments. In fact, only four out of 10 people know who preached the Sermon on the Mount. Of those polled 81 percent of born-again Christians think that "God helps them that help themselves" is a direct quote from the Bible rather than from Benjamin Franklin.

Other research by Gary M. Burge revealed that fully 80 percent of high school students at strong evangelical churches don't know where to find the Lord's Prayer.

Burge also found that more than 50 percent of high school students think that the cities of Sodom and Gomorrah were husband and wife.

Such widespread biblical illiteracy bodes poorly for the future of strong nations and a morally sensitive world. We need to learn or relearn the great stories of

OPENING BLACK & WHITE DRAWING
Every story will open with a delightful little black and white pencil drawing by Darrel Tank.

THE BIBLE STORIES
These Bible stories for school-age children were especially written for this new series by Ruth Redding Brand. The stories are all written at a fifth-grade reading level and are designed to be read by children ages 9 through 12.

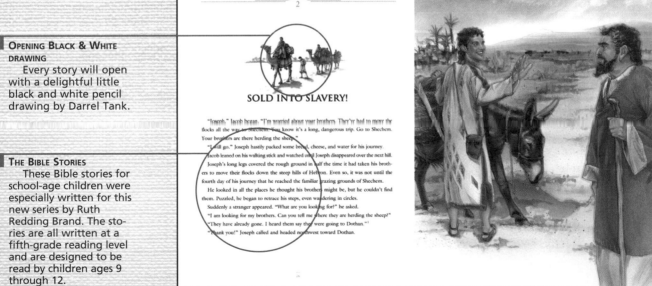

PHOTOGRAPHS
These photos of modern sites in Bible lands tie the stories to the same Holy Land that children see on the news each evening.

THE BIBLE TEXT
At the bottom of the second spread of each story, are the actual Bible verses on which the story is based. We put them at the bottom of the page because they are the foundation on which the whole series of books is based.

STORIES FOR PRESCHOOLERS
These delightful little one-page stories are actually condensed versions of the longer story—written for preschoolers, ages 2-5, and using simple language to retell the same Bible story for little ones.

the Bible. They will help us know how to set our ethical and spiritual compasses.

The first of the three words, "Family," tells us that the content of this book is geared for the entire family and not just for one age group. How often, for example, have you as a parent become bored by reading stories—cute and clever as they may be—written specifically for a child? And so this book has something for all members of your family, which explains why at first glance the layout appears to be confusing.

Ruth Redding Brand has written the **centerpiece stories** for elementary-age children. The stories have a relatively controlled vocabulary and a carefully crafted sentence structure, which places them at a fifth-grade readability level. If your children are in the fourth or fifth or sixth grades, they'll be able to read these stories by themselves. If they're a bit younger, they'll understand the stories when you read them aloud.

Not only that, but your children will find the

material in the **glossary** especially interesting. Why? Because the glossary is packed with trivia, which fascinates children of all age groups. They'll delight in learning, for instance, not only how to pronounce the biblical place and personal names in English but also how to pronounce them in the original Hebrew, Babylonian, Egyptian, Greek, etc. The key for the **pronunciation guide** has been made as simple as possible by Leona Glidden Running, a specialist in ancient Near Eastern languages.

The brief **description** of each scriptural place and person mentioned in the stories retold in this book features facts that even teenagers and adults will find informative. The glossary is very much like a concise Bible dictionary.

The **Bible bedtime story,** which ends each chapter, is a condensed version of the centerpiece story. It has been especially written for preschool children. Elements in the main story that might be especially frightening for toddlers have been either toned down or omitted. The story itself is short—about 300 words. Little children won't get restless as they listen to the story. The mode of discourse is simple and straightforward. Beginning readers will find that these stories make good practice reading.

The **Bible passage** in the drop deck of each story is from the *International Children's Bible*. The preface to that version states: "It is the first translation of the Holy Scriptures prepared specifically for children." It's "the only version that [can] be comprehended on a third-grade instructional level." The inclusion of the biblical passages behind each story assures young readers that author Brand didn't make up these stories; they are biblically based.

The **timeline** that appears at the beginning of this book will help teenagers and adults see where a particular set of stories fits into the overall chronology of historical events as well as how it fits into a chronology of biblical events. As a result, these timelines, prepared by Constance Clark Gane, an authority in ancient Near Eastern history, may refer to events that

took place in China, Africa, or the Americas at about the same time as the biblical event narrated in the centerpiece story.

The **illustrations** will have a wide appeal. Elementary-age children will resonate with the original paintings, done especially for the Family Bible Story project. The illustrators have been coached to make elements in the illustrations authentic. The photographs of biblical places and artifacts will especially appeal to adult readers.

Captions provide young adults with information that doesn't appear within the centerpiece story itself. In other words, the captions serve a useful purpose and don't merely repeat something the story writer has already said.

The sections labeled **Did You Know?** generally will appeal more to young adults and adults than to children. The vocabulary is not limited, and the topics and the level of discourse are often best suited for more mature readers.

As you can see, the various elements that constitute this book truly make it the Family Bible Story.

• Joseph sold into slavery
(1898 B.C.)
• Jacob goes to Haran (1929 B.C.) • Isaac dies (1886 B.C.)
• Jacob marries Leah & Rachel • Joseph given high position
(1922 B.C.) (1885 B.C.)
• Joseph born (1915 B.C.) • Jacob and family move to
• Jacob & family move Egypt (1876 B.C.)
• Jacob born (2006 B.C.) to Canaan (1909 B.C.) • Jacob dies (1859 B.C.) • Joseph dies (1805 B.C.)

B.C. **2000** / / / **1950** / / / **1900** / / / **1850** / / / **1800**

• EUROPE—"the Beaker • Egypt—Wine imported from • Mesopotamia—Earliest known • Mesopotamia— Babylonians
People" migrate from Crete legal decision—a murder case invent multiplication tables
Spain to S. Germany, former • China—Domestication of pig • Palestine—Middle Bronze IIA • China—October 16, 1876 B.C.
Czecho-Slovakia and England • Mesopotamia— Astrology • China—Erlitou on the Yellow earliest recorded eclipse
• Egypt—Middle Kingdom developed in Babylonia River, first known city in China (reign of King Zhong Kong,
(c. 2040-1730 B.C.) Yang Shao in N.W. Honan Xia Dynasty)
• Egypt—First bronze work
in Egypt

JOSEPH

Joseph was the son of Jacob and Rachel. Jacob made him a special garment that his brothers envied. When Joseph dreamed that his family would give him deference, the jealousy mushroomed. Later his brothers sold him for 20 silver shekels. In Egypt Potiphar bought Joseph. When Joseph interpreted a dream for Pharaoh, the Egyptian king made him second in command.

JACOB

Jacob was the son of Isaac and Rebekah and the twin of Esau. His name meant "he supplants" or "he takes by the heel." Later God changed his name to Israel. Jacob was the progenitor of the Hebrew (Israelite) people. He died at age 147 and was later buried in the Cave of Machpelah, bought by Abraham for Sarah's burial.

BROTHERS

Joseph had 11 brothers and one sister. His brothers names are Asher, Benjamin, Dan, Gad, Issachar, Judah, Levi, Naphtali, Reuben, Simeon, and Zebulun. Only one was his full brother, Benjamin. The others were half-brothers, born to Jacob's other wife, Leah, and to his two concubines. The tribes of Israel took their names from this family. The sister's name was Dinah.

PHARAOH

This Egyptian title for their kings meant "great house." The term originally referred to the palace where the kings lived, but from the Eighteenth Dynasty on (the time of Moses) it became a title that referred to the king himself. According to ancient Egyptian mythology, upon death the pharaoh became the god Osiris and went to join the other deities.

"Hear, I pray you, this dream . . ."

Genesis 37:6

STRANGE DREAMS

Joseph ran his hands over the smooth cloth of his new robe. Ever since he could remember, he had received a beautiful new cloak from his father even before he had outgrown his old one.

"Thank you, Father," he said with a big smile as he paraded back and forth in front of Jacob. "This robe is the most beautiful yet!" The robe reached to his ankles and encircled the full length of his arms in folds of fabric. Brightly woven designs of red and blue marched down the front of the robe and danced around its hem. On each shoulder and across the chest, gold embroidery sparkled in the sunlight.

"All ready for work, I see!" sneered Naphtali as he stepped out of a shadow. Disgusted and jealous, he walked away.

Neither Joseph nor his father paid much attention to Naphtali.

Jacob's eyes lit with love as he looked at his handsome son, dressed like a prince in royal clothing. Now 17 years old, Joseph's quick, dazzling smile and flashing eyes constantly reminded Jacob of the wife he had loved and lost, for Rachel had died when little Benjamin was born.

"As long as I have Joseph," Jacob murmured to himself, "I still have Rachel."

But Jacob loved Joseph not only because he reminded him of Rachel, but also because Joseph, of all his sons, tried to honor the one true God. Joseph was also eager to please his father. In fact, Jacob had begun to depend on him to let him know what his other sons were doing, for it seemed that they were always getting into trouble of some kind.

Joseph told his father everything he knew about his half brothers' schemes and mischief. But as Jacob urged them to do better, they only resented Joseph more and more. They glared at him, growled at him, and cursed him when Jacob was out of earshot.

"You overdressed tattletale!" they fumed. "Someday Father isn't going to be around to rescue you, and then—!" They left the threat unfinished, but their clenched fists spoke more loudly than words.

Jacob had two wives—Leah and Rachel—and two secondary wives—Zilpah and Bilhah. Altogether they had 12 sons and one daughter. Sibling rivalry made this family dysfunctional.

GENESIS 37:2-11

Joseph was a young man, 17 years old. He and his brothers cared for the flocks. His brothers were the sons of Bilhah and Zilpah, his father's wives. Joseph gave his father bad reports about his brothers. Joseph was born when his father Israel, also called Jacob, was old. Israel loved Joseph more than his other sons. He made Joseph a special robe with long sleeves. Joseph's brothers saw that their father loved Joseph more than he loved them. So they hated their brother and could not speak to him politely.

One time Joseph had a dream. When he told his brothers about it, they hated him even more. Joseph said, "Listen to the dream I had. We were in the field tying bundles of wheat together. My bundle stood up, and your bundles of wheat gathered around mine. Your

Joseph hardly listened to his brothers' angry words. As his father's favorite child, he felt that no harm could ever come to him. Besides, he reasoned, shouldn't he try to help his father correct these dreadful half brothers of his?

With every day that passed, Jacob's sons grew angrier and angrier. "You know he's going to pass every one of us by, and give the birthright to Joseph, don't you?" suggested Reuben. As the oldest son, he had forfeited his right to the birthright long ago by an evil deed, but he felt that Simeon should have it, or if not Simeon, anyone but Joseph!

"Yeah," muttered the brothers, their faces dark as a dust storm, "that brat thinks he's better than we are, and Father lets him get away with lording it over us!"

"By the way," Zebulun asked, in mock innocence, "when was the last time Father gave you a robe fit for royalty?"

A chorus of bitter laughter greeted his question.

"I'd sure like to teach 'little brother' a lesson!" snarled Levi. "He wouldn't think he was so pretty or so smart when I got through with him!"

"Well, I guess you know what would happen to you if Father ever found out about it, don't you?" added Gad, with an unpleasant little laugh. The brothers didn't answer, but each of them thought fearfully of not getting any inheritance from Jacob.

That night the brothers gathered their flocks together, ready for the next day's big shearing festival. Joseph worked with Bilhah's and Zilpah's sons, his half brothers Dan, Naphtali, Gad, and Asher. For this special occasion even Jacob rode out to the fields. Now past his working days, Jacob still wanted to keep an eye on things.

Before day had broken the next morning, the brothers were bustling about. Judah and Issachar gathered sticks and stubble to start a fire. As the fire started to blaze and the moon faded from the sky, Joseph suddenly stood before them and held up a hand.

"Listen!" he commanded, a smile touching his lips. As the flickering firelight danced across Joseph's finely chiseled features, even his brothers couldn't help thinking, for a moment, that he looked like a carved statue of a god, or at least visiting royalty. But the thought quickly vanished as they listened to Joseph's words.

"Last night," Joseph began, his gaze shifting from one brother to the next, "I had a dream. We were in the field tying bundles of wheat together." He paused as he saw his brothers' faces, curious in spite of themselves. "My bundle stood up, and your bundles of wheat gathered around mine. Your bundles bowed down to mine."[1]

> "SOMEDAY FATHER ISN'T GOING TO BE AROUND TO RESCUE YOU, AND THEN—!"

bundles bowed down to mine."
His brothers said, "Do you really think you will be king over us? Do you truly think you will rule over us?" His brothers hated him even more now. They hated him because of his dreams and what he had said.
Then Joseph had another dream. He told his brothers about it also. He said, "Listen, I had another dream. I saw the sun, moon, and 11 stars bowing down to me."
Joseph also told his father about this dream. But his father scolded him, saying, "What kind of dream is this? Do you really believe that your mother, your brothers and I will bow down to you?" Joseph's brothers were jealous of him. But his father thought about what all these things could mean.

JOSEPH'S COAT

A roar of angry voices met his words, and only the thought of Jacob, still sleeping in a nearby tent, kept them from rushing upon him.

"So, you think you're going to be a king, or that you're going to rule over us?" the brothers shouted, nearly beside themselves with anger and resentment. *"Never, little brother, never!"*

Joseph worked silently all day, rounding up the sheep and guiding them one at a time into one of the narrow chutes his brothers had built of stones. Zebulun, Gad, Simeon, and Asher also guided sheep into chutes, where other brothers waited to catch them.

As Joseph's sheep ran down the chute, Levi's strong arms grabbed it and flipped it to its back. With experienced hands Levi soon cut away its thick wool coat. With a complaining "Baaaa!" the sheep, feeling suddenly light and frisky, bounded away and began to graze.

As Joseph headed one sheep after another into the chute, his mind kept toying with the strange dream he'd had the night before. He remembered stories his father had told him of a dream God had given him, and of God speaking to his grandmother Rebekah and his grandfather Isaac and his great-grandfather Abraham. Had God been telling him something in this dream? If so, what was God trying to tell him?

The expression used for Joseph's robe *(kethoneth passīm)* is extremely rare.

When odd expressions appear, biblical scholars (1) try to figure out the root word(s), (2) compare other uses of the same term in the same language, (3) analyze the context, (4) review cognate languages for similar words, and (5) examine ancient Near Eastern pictures.

1. Root Words—Root meanings don't help much with the *kethoneth passīm* that Joseph wore.

The word *kethoneth* is not especially mysterious. It refers to a kind of underclothing that sometimes had sleeves and sometimes reached to the ankles.

It is the word *passīm* that is puzzling.

P. Kyle McCarter, Jr., thinks the root for *passīm* refers to fingers and toes. Since the usual *kethoneth* did not have long sleeves and did not reach the feet, this particular garment would be extraordinary.

2. Other Hebrew Usage—Only one other time the same two words are used—in 2 Samuel 13:18, 19. The person wearing the *kethoneth passīm* in this story is Princess Tamar, daughter of King David. This only confuses the matter. Was Joseph wearing women's clothing?

3. The Context—The rest of both stories do not help us understand what the *kethoneth passīm* looked like. All we can infer from the context is that it was probably a special piece of clothing.

4. Cognate Languages—E. A. Speiser has pointed out that certain ancient Mesopotamian texts refer to a garment called *kutinnū* (sometimes *kitû*) *pišanu*. As you can see, the words *kutinnū pišanu* faintly resemble the Hebrew words *kethoneth passīm*. It is not impossible that they refer to the same garment.

What did the *kutinnū pišanu* look like? It was a piece of clothing sometimes thrown around the shoulders of a statue of a goddess. In short, it was a female garment.

Furthermore, it had *pišanu*—medallions—affixed to it. Sometimes they fell off and had to be put back on by a special tailor.

5. Ancient Near Eastern Pictures—Certain monuments portray people wearing what archaeologists identify as *kethoneths*. The garment was not limited to a particular culture, but was worn by people from various nations. But we don't know that we have pictures of a *kethoneth passīm*.

So the mystery remains.

ART LANDERMAN

That night Joseph threw himself on a sheepskin in a tent next to his father's. His back ached from bending over sheep all day, and he fell into a sound sleep. But as he slept he dreamed that he floated effortlessly and fearlessly in a star-studded sky. He felt like Joseph, but a different Joseph, one who traveled in a distant, dazzling world he'd never seen before, yet one in which he felt at home.

Even as he gazed at the sparkling expanse of space, 11 stars suddenly blazed into greater brilliance and streaked toward him. At the same time, the sun and the moon burst out of the darkness and flashed across the blackness of space to join the 11 stars. Joseph gazed in wonder as the dazzling lights surrounded him and bowed low before him. Then he woke up.

"Father! Gad! Asher!" he called as he sprang from his sheepskin bedding and bolted from the tent. "Oh, everyone!" he cried, too excited to think or care that it was still the middle of the night.

Rumpled forms staggered into the circle around the still-smoldering fire. "What's the matter with you?" a rough voice asked.

Jacob, favoring his stiff hip, limped into sight. "Yes, my boy, what is it? What's wrong?"

Joseph's eyes flashed with excitement, and the words tumbled from his lips as he tried to explain the strange, beautiful, wonderful things he had seen. But the words he spoke carried no vision of streaking stars, dazzling sun, and glowing moon. The brothers heard only "Eleven stars and the sun and moon bowed down to me." The hot blood pounded in their heads as they listened to yet another of Joseph's dreams in which he set himself up as a ruler over them!

Even Jacob lost his patience with Joseph. "What kind of dream is this? Do you really believe that your mother, your brothers and I will bow down to you?" [2]

Muttering darkly, the brothers stumbled back to their tents, only to find themselves too angry to go back to sleep.

Joseph returned to his tent, hurting from his father's rebuke but dismissing his brothers' reactions as just another example of their bad tempers. But the dream stayed with him, and he wondered again, Is God trying to tell me something?

Jacob lay back down, his eyes wide and staring into the darkness. Had he encouraged Joseph to dream such wild things by spoiling him and dressing him like a prince? Or did these dreams mean something? If so, what could they possibly mean? Jacob wondered and worried.

---

[1] Genesis 37:6, ICB.
[2] Verse 10, ICB.

Sheep in Bible times had fat tails that grew very large and heavy, often dragging on the ground. The breed is now called Awassi.

Strange Dreams

"Joseph has a new coat!" Dan grumbled to Asher as they took care of the sheep one morning. "Why doesn't Papa ever give us coats like Joseph's?"

Asher looked across the field at Joseph. Asher wiped the sweat off his forehead with the back of his hand. "I don't know," he answered. "It's not fair. And Joseph always tells Papa whenever we do any little thing wrong. Papa loves him best, but I *hate* Joseph!"

All Joseph's big brothers were jealous of him. And it was true—their papa did love Joseph better than any of his other children.

"I had a funny dream last night," Joseph told his brothers one morning. "I dreamed we were tying up bundles of wheat in the field. My bundle stood up, and all your bundles bowed down to mine."

Joseph's brothers did not think it was a funny dream at all! "Do you think you are going to be our king?" they shouted. "We will never bow down to you!" And they hated Joseph more than ever.

Soon Joseph had another dream, and again he told his family all about it. "I dreamed that the sun, the moon, and 11 stars bowed down to me," he said.

"What do you mean?" his papa scolded. "Do you think all of us will really bow down before you?"

Joseph's dreams made his brothers even more angry with him. But Papa Jacob thought about those dreams. Were they just ordinary dreams, or was God trying to tell them something? Papa Jacob remembered when God had spoken to him. He knew that God had spoken to his own father, Isaac. He knew that God had spoken to his grandfather Abraham. Did God have a special message for his son Joseph, too?

—LINDA PORTER CARLYLE

SOLD INTO SLAVERY!

"Joseph," Jacob began, "I'm worried about your brothers. They've had to move the flocks all the way to Shechem. You know it's a long, dangerous trip. Go to Shechem. Your brothers are there herding the sheep."

"I will go." Joseph hastily packed some bread, cheese, and water for his journey.

Jacob leaned on his walking stick and watched until Joseph disappeared over the next hill.

Joseph's long legs covered the rough ground in half the time it had taken his brothers to move their flocks down the steep hills of Hebron. Even so, it was not until the fourth day of his journey that he reached the familiar grazing grounds of Shechem.

He looked in all the places he thought his brothers might be, but he couldn't find them. Puzzled, he began to retrace his steps, even wandering in circles.

Suddenly a stranger appeared. "What are you looking for?" he asked.

"I am looking for my brothers. Can you tell me where they are herding the sheep?"

"They have already gone. I heard them say they were going to Dothan."[1]

"Thank you!" Joseph called and headed northwest toward Dothan.

Joseph walked nearly 50 miles to Shechem. Then he hiked another 15 miles to Dothan, where sheep still graze today, as in this photograph.

company's coming?" he suggested with a nasty gleam in his eye. "I think we ought to have a little welcome party for the great dreamer!"

The closer Joseph came to his half brothers, the angrier they grew. Mocking words turned to threats of violence, until finally one voice sliced through the air with the words "Let's kill him!"

"Good idea," they all roared. "Let's throw his body into one of the wells. We can tell our father that a wild animal killed him. Then we will see what will become of his dreams." [2] Reuben felt strangely uneasy. As the oldest, he would be held responsible if any harm came to Joseph.

"Let's not kill him," Reuben argued. "Throw him into this well here in the desert. But don't hurt him!" Secretly he thought, I'll come back later when no one's looking and get Joseph out of the pit!

They all agreed to do as Reuben suggested. So as Joseph neared them, they grabbed him and ripped off the beautiful robe his father had given him.

In Dothan, Joseph's brothers squatted on the ground, watching the sheep graze peacefully. Dan tugged Simeon's sleeve as he spotted an approaching figure. "Someone's coming!"

Simeon peered at the distant form, then suddenly stood up. A deep red crept up his neck and spread across his face. "It's Joseph!" He spat out the words as if they had a bad taste. "Come to spy on us, probably! Why don't you go over to the south slope where Reuben and Levi are working and tell them

> "LET'S NOT KILL HIM," REUBEN ARGUED. "THROW HIM INTO THIS WELL HERE IN THE DESERT. BUT DON'T HURT HIM!"

"You dreamer!" they snarled in his face. "Let's see how many of your dreams come true now!" And they hurled him to the bottom of a cistern, deep, dark, and dry.

Joseph landed violently, his head and right shoulder slamming into the wall of the cistern. Pain knifed through his head and back, and he lay still, the breath knocked out of him.

GENESIS 37:12-33

One day Joseph's brothers went to Shechem to herd their father's sheep. Jacob said to Joseph, "Go to Shechem. Your brothers are there hearding the sheep."

Joseph answered, "I will go."

His father said, "Go and see if your brothers and the sheep are all right. Then come back and tell me."

When Joseph came to Shechem, a man found him wandering in the field. He asked Joseph, "What are you looking for?"

Joseph answered, "I am looking for my brothers. Can yout ell me where they are herding the sheep?" The man said, ". . . I heard them say they were going to Dothan." So Joseph . . . found them in Dothan. . . .

Before he reached them, they made a plan to kill him. They said to each other,

His brothers' voices drifted down to him as they laughed, making crude jokes. For the first time Joseph began to realize how much his half brothers hated him.

Soon Joseph smelled the faint aroma of bubbling stew. His brothers' boisterous laughter and loud voices reached his ears as they smacked their lips over their supper. Tired and hungry after his long journey, Joseph huddled in the darkness.

Hot tears stung his eyes, but he brushed them away impatiently. Surely this was nothing more than a cruel joke! Surely his brothers would not leave him here to die!

Soon Joseph heard a babble of voices, and the harsh and lusty complaints of many camels. A caravan had arrived!

"What will we gain if we kill our brother and hide his death? Let's sell him to these Ishmaelites. . . . After all, he is our brother,

Cisterns (the Hebrew word means well or cistern) were bottle-shaped chambers cut into the limestone bedrock to collect rain run-off.

our own flesh and blood," Judah said.[4]

"All right, we'll do it your way!" the others agreed.

Suddenly Joseph felt the hard knot of a rope hit the side of his head and a rough voice (he thought it

"Here comes that dreamer. Let's kill him. . . . We can tell our father that a wild animal killed him. Then we will see what will become of his dreams." . . .

[Reuben] said, ". . . Throw him into this well here in the desert. . . ." Reuben planned to save Joseph later. . . . When

Joseph came to his brothers, they pulled off his robe with long sleeves. Then they threw him into the well. . . . There was no water in it. . . .

The brothers sat down to eat. When they looked up, they saw a group of Ishmaelites. They were traveling . . . to Egypt. . . . Judah

said . . ., ". . . Let's sell [Joseph]. . . ." When the . . . traders came by, the brothers took Joseph out of the well. They sold him . . . for eight ounces of silver. . . . The Ishmaelites took him to Egypt. . . .

When Reuben came back to the well, Joseph was not there.

was Levi's) call, "Grab hold of that rope!"

Painfully Joseph held onto the rope while his brothers hauled him to the surface. He blinked in the sunlight, and then stared at the traders who had stopped to talk with his brothers.

The Ishmaelites turned to examine Joseph as his brothers shoved him roughly into their midst. "So this is the lad," they murmured, squeezing the muscles in his arms and thumping him on his back.

"He's young, well built, but not used to a lot of work, I'll wager," one of the traders commented as he examined Joseph's hands. "He'll soon get toughened up in Egypt, though!

"I'll give you five ounces of silver for him!" the trader offered.

"Twelve! We're selling you this boy, not giving him away!" Judah protested. "We've got to get at least 12 ounces of silver for him!"

The trader eyed him narrowly. "I'll give you eight. Take it or leave it!"

"He's yours," Judah replied, all business. "You've got yourself a slave!" And he watched as the trader weighed the silver—just eight ounces—and placed it in his outstretched hand.

Joseph's heart beat wildly. Could he be dreaming? But the rough hands that grabbed him and tied his hands behind his back definitely felt real. He almost choked as someone tied another rope around his neck, then lashed the other end of it to a camel's saddle.

A command rang out, and the caravan lurched into motion. The sudden movement nearly yanked Joseph's head from his shoulders, but as he stumbled along after the caravan, his brothers' heartless laughter hurt more than the ropeburn on his neck.

Then he thought of his father, and the tears rolled down his cheeks. "Dear God," he prayed, "comfort

The Ishmaelites were not-so-distant cousins of Jacob's clan—descendants from Ishmael's 12 sons. The offspring of Ishmael's son Qedar became camel trainers and may have been the merchants who bought Joseph.

Without modern scientific methods of blood-typing, Jacob would have had no way of knowing that the blood on Joseph's robe was from a goat.

air and neatly caught it on his shepherd's rod—"and dip it in blood and show it to Father. He'll think a wild animal killed Joseph!"

Issachar had hardly finished speaking before the brothers seized a goat and slaughtered it. With careless hands they dipped Joseph's tunic in the blood. They smeared the gold-embroidered shoulders and the red-and-blue torso and the hem in the goat's blood. Then they trailed the whole garment once more through a pool of blood.

Back home, days later, they showed the coat to Jacob, who began trembling as if suddenly struck with a disease, while his shocked eyes tried vainly to tear themselves away from Joseph's blood-smeared coat.

"My son Joseph has been torn to pieces!" he moaned and rocked back and forth, back and forth. Tearing off his clothes and putting on rough garments made from grain sacks, he cried, "I will be sad about my son until the day I die."[6]

Jacob's sons were alarmed at the intensity of their father's grief and tried to comfort him. All of Jacob's family offered him love and comfort, but no one could console the old man. As the days passed, his sons feared that even though they had not killed Joseph, they might yet bear the guilt of seeing their father die from grief.

my father and please let us see each other again!"

Just as the caravan pulled out of sight, Reuben returned from the field and hurried to the place where Joseph had been thrown into the cistern. Standing at the edge of the pit, he peered into the blackness below. Joseph was gone!

Racing to his brothers, he cried, "The boy is not there! What will I do?"[5]

Their strange silence soon told him they knew of Joseph's fate. In fear and sorrow Reuben tore his clothes, a sign of great distress. Then the other brothers knew Reuben had planned to rescue Joseph, but Reuben didn't care. "What am I going to do now?" he moaned.

"Well," Issachar suggested, "we could simply take Joseph's fancy coat here"—he tossed the coat into the

---

[1] Genesis 37:15-17, ICB.

[2] Verse 20, ICB.

[3] Verse 21, ICB.

[4] Verse 27, ICB.

[5] Verse 30, ICB.

[6] Verses 33-35, ICB.

Sold Into Slavery!

"Go, check on your brothers," Papa Jacob said to Joseph. "They have been gone a long time. Then come back and tell me how they are and how the sheep are getting along."

"OK," Joseph answered cheerfully. He packed some food for his trip and started out.

"Look who's coming!" the brothers shouted to each other when they saw Joseph in the distance. "It's that dreamer!" And they hated Joseph so much that they talked about killing him.

"No, let's not kill him," the oldest brother, Reuben, said. "Let's just throw him into that deep hole in the ground." (Reuben had a secret plan. He would come back later and rescue Joseph.)

So the brothers grabbed Joseph as he came into their camp. They pulled off his beautiful coat and threw him into the pit.

Just as they sat down to eat their dinner, the brothers saw traders coming, riding on tall camels. "Let's not kill Joseph," Judah said. "After all, he is our brother. Let's sell him to those traders. Then he will be gone, but he won't be dead."

"Good idea!" the other brothers agreed. So they sold Joseph to the traders to be a slave.

Then the brothers killed a goat and dipped Joseph's beautiful coat in the blood. When they went home, they showed the coat to Papa Jacob.

"Oh, no!" Papa Jacob cried. "A wild animal has attacked Joseph and eaten him!" Papa Jacob cried and cried for his favorite son for many, many days. His family tried to comfort him, but he would only shake his head and moan, "I will die of sadness for my son." And then he cried again.

The brothers had gotten rid of Joseph as they wanted to, but they had made their father very sad.

—LINDA PORTER CARLYLE

POTIPHAR'S SLAVE, PRISON'S PROPHET

A miserable group of people—men, women, and children—huddled together under the hot Egyptian sun, waiting to be sold to the highest bidder. The Ishmaelite traders eagerly pushed Joseph forward, because he would be sold next.

"Ah, we've got a real prize here!" shouted the auctioneer, pointing to Joseph. "This one's young enough to learn, but old enough to work hard!"

A roar of boisterous laughter greeted his words, and the bidding began.

On the far edge of the crowd stood a man with an air of authority. Quietly he signaled to a bidder near the front of the crowd. Joseph saw the distant man lift his hand, palm up. From watching other sales, Joseph guessed what that meant—no limit; pay whatever you have to, but buy him. Joseph was sold so quickly it surprised him.

He soon learned that the man who bought him was Potiphar, captain of the palace guard. The official said something in the Egyptian language to Joseph, but Joseph did not understand Egyptian. Then he understood that his new master wanted to know his name. Joseph pointed to himself and said clearly, "Yoh-SAYF."

"YOHsip," Potiphar repeated.

Joseph marveled at Potiphar's mud-brick house with its many rooms. It even had a staircase to the second floor. The house was located within a walled courtyard with a

reflecting pool. Inside the house Joseph noticed furniture to sleep in and sit on. This place was nothing like his Canaan tent-home. Joseph listened carefully to everything anyone said, and soon began picking up a few Egyptian words. Soon he knew how to speak the Egyptian language.

Potiphar assigned Joseph to work in his bakery. Quickly Joseph mastered each task. He carried grain, mixed the flour with water, and baked all the many different breads and pastries known to the Egyptians. When new slaves came into the bakery, Joseph taught them all he knew and helped organize their work.

Potiphar heard what a good worker Joseph was. *I could use someone like that to handle my household accounts and keep everything running smoothly!* he said to himself.

THE TEMPTATION

One day Potiphar declared, "YOHsip, from now on you will supervise my household staff and all my business. You're the best manager I've ever seen."

Joseph liked working in Potiphar's large, beautiful home. But at night he thought about his own tent-home and his father Jacob, and a lonely feeling formed a lump in his throat. Then he would look at the stars peeking in through the small windows at the top of the wall of his room and think, *Those same*

"COME ON, YOHSIP," SHE SAID ONE DAY. "NO ONE IS AROUND TO SEE WHAT WE DO."

---

stars shine over Father's tent, and the same God watches over us.

Joseph worked hard to keep Potiphar's trust. But one person made his job difficult, and that was Potiphar's wife. Day after day she tried to get Joseph to pay attention to her instead of doing his job. She even tried to persuade Joseph to love her as if he were her husband!

"Come on, YOHsip," she said one day. "No one is around to see what we do."

"My master," Joseph answered respectfully, but firmly, "trusts me with everything in his house. He has put me in charge of everything he owns. There is no one in his house greater than I. He has not kept anything from me, except you. And that is because you are his wife. How can I do such an evil thing? It is a sin against God."[1]

But Potiphar's wife paid no attention to Joseph's words. With a giggle she grabbed Joseph's loincloth. He pulled away from her and ran out the door, leaving his garment in her hands.

Now she was angry. She began to scream.

Servants came running from everywhere—all but Joseph, of course.

"What's wrong?" they asked.

"Get my husband! Get my husband!" she shrieked.

When Potiphar appeared, his wife threw herself at

GENESIS 39:1–40:23

[Potiphar] bought Joseph from the Ishmaelites. . . . [Potiphar] saw that the Lord made Joseph successful in everything. . . .

So Potiphar was very happy with Joseph. . . . He put Joseph in charge of the house. . . .

After some time the wife of Joseph's master began to desire Joseph. . . .

One day Joseph went into the house to do his work as usual. He was the only man in the house at that time. His master's wife grabbed his coat. She said to him, "Come and have sexual relations with me." But

Joseph left his coat in her hand and ran out of the house. . . .

She called to the servants. . . . She said, " . . . [This Hebrew slave] . . . came in and tried to have sexual relations with me. But I screamed. . . . He ran away. But he left his coat with me." . . .

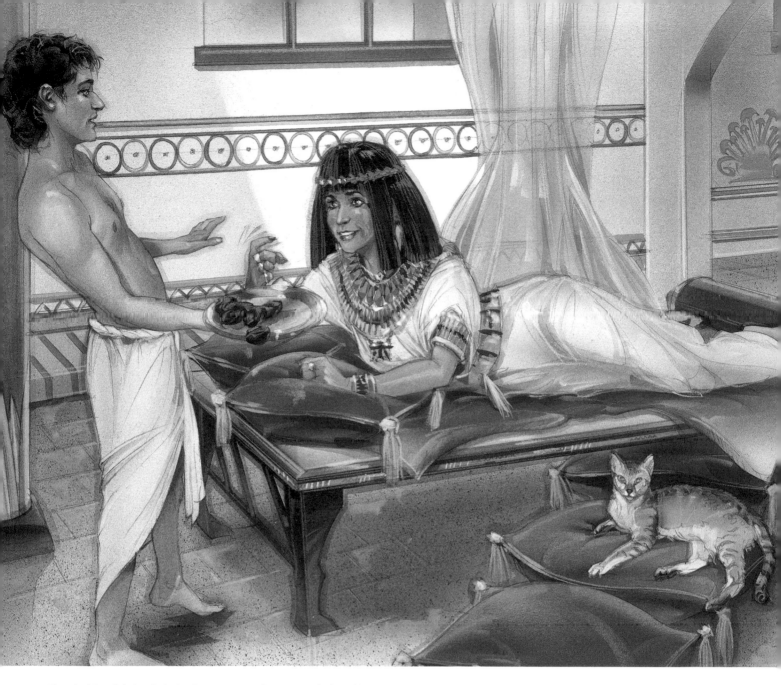

The clothing fabric of choice in Egypt was linen. Loincloths of heavy linen were for men. Some women wore form-fitting dresses of see-through linen.

him, sobbing and wailing. "This Hebrew slave you brought here came in to shame me! When he came near me, I screamed. He ran away."[2] Her eyes rolled wildly and she sobbed loudly, but Potiphar noticed that no tears fell.

Inwardly he groaned. He didn't believe for a

So Potiphar arrested Joseph and put him into prison. This prison was where the king's prisoners were put. . . .

But the Lord was with Joseph. . . . The Lord caused the prison warden to like Joseph. . . .

Two of the king's officers displeased the king. The officers were the man who served wine to the king and the king's baker. . . . So he put them in . . . prison. . . . This was the same prison where Joseph was kept. . . .

One night both . . . had a dream. . . . When Joseph came to them the next morning, he saw they were worried. Joseph asked . . . , "Why do you look so unhappy today?" The two men answered, "We both had dreams last night. But no one can explain the meaning of them to us." Joseph said to them, "God is the only One who can explain the meaning of dreams. So tell me your dreams."

minute that his slave had done anything wrong, but he certainly could not call his wife a liar in front of all the servants. What a dilemma!

Turning to his guards, he directed, "Throw YOHsip in prison!"

There! He'd done it, but he'd lost the best business manager he'd ever had, all because of his wife's foolishness and lies.

The dungeon in which Joseph found himself offered no light or comfort, only gloomy rooms crowded with prisoners. Metal chains around his ankles bit into his flesh. Carrying mud and straw with the other prisoners to make bricks, Joseph worked under the watchful eye and ready whip of an overseer. At night Joseph slumped to the hard dirt floor, grateful for rest among the fleas, lice, and mosquitoes.

Canaan seemed far away and long ago. Had he really been the pampered son of an important man? Had he once worn a beautiful coat instead of a filthy rag? But as Joseph listened to the groans of the men around him, his heart softened. Some of them had committed crimes and deserved punishment, but some, he felt sure, were as innocent as he.

Little by little Joseph made friends with the prisoners. Day by day they learned to trust him with their problems.

In time the director of the prison, Potiphar, Joseph's former employer, learned to depend on Joseph. He trusted him so much that he put him in charge of the prison. "The Lord made Joseph successful in everything he did."[3]

Two prisoners especially interested Joseph. One had been the king's cupbearer. The other had been the chief baker for the palace.

One morning Joseph noticed that the two men looked troubled.

"Why do you look so unhappy today?" he asked.

"We both had dreams last night," they answered.

The well-dressed Egyptian man or woman often wore a wig. At home, wigs were stored on stands and coiffed by servants. The wig in this photograph is made of human hair and of excellent craftsmanship. The curly hair at the crown had been soaked in beeswax and resin.

"But no one can explain the meaning of them to us."

"God is the only One who can explain the meaning of dreams. So tell me your dreams," Joseph responded.

"Well," the cupbearer began, "I dreamed I saw a vine. On the vine there were three branches. I watched the branches bud and blossom, and then the grapes ripened." The cupbearer's eyes grew big with wonder as he remembered what he had seen. No one had ever seen nature move so quickly before! "I was holding the king's cup. So I took the grapes and squeezed the juice into the cup. Then I gave it to the king." He stopped and looked at Joseph.

Some 300 years before Joseph lived, the Egyptians enjoyed 15 different kinds of bread. A few hundred years later they baked about 40 kinds of bread.

In a flash God revealed to Joseph what the dream meant. Without hesitating, he said to the cupbearer, "The three branches stand for three days. Before the end of three days the king will free you. He will allow you to return to your work."

Joseph paused, then asked softly, "But when you are free, remember me. Be kind to me. Tell the king about me so that I can get out of this prison."[4]

The cupbearer beamed and nodded his head. "Oh, yes! Yes, of course! I'll remember you, Joseph!"

By now the baker was tugging at Joseph's arm. "What about my dream, Joseph? I also had a dream. I dreamed there were three bread baskets on my head. In the top basket there were all kinds of baked food for the king. But the birds were eating this food out of the basket on my head." Joseph had such good news for the cupbearer; surely he'd have good news for the baker, also.

A shadow flickered across Joseph's face, and he looked soberly into the baker's eyes.

"The three baskets stand for three days. Before the end of three days, the king will cut off your head! He will hang your body on a pole. And the birds will eat your flesh."[5]

The baker stared at Joseph with horror-filled eyes, then turned and disappeared into a gloomy corner, his chain clanking behind him.

A day went by. Another day passed. On the third day prison guards threw open the gate. "The king's cupbearer!" the guard called, and the cupbearer, smiling broadly, left the prison without so much as a backward glance at Joseph.

"The king's chief baker!" the guard called, and the baker stumbled from the prison, but turned as he left to look at Joseph with fear-glazed eyes.

Soon word drifted back to the remaining prisoners. The cupbearer had been reinstated. But the baker had been beheaded and hanged in the public square, where birds flocked to his lifeless body to prey on his flesh.

And Joseph still remained a prisoner, far from home. The cupbearer forgot all about him. But God had not forgotten.

[1] Genesis 39:8, 9, ICB.
[2] Verses 17, 18, ICB.
[3] Verse 23, ICB.
[4] Genesis 40:7-14, ICB.
[5] Verses 16-19, ICB.

Potiphar's Slave, Prison's Prophet

When the traders reached Egypt, they sold Joseph there as a slave. An important man named Potiphar bought him.

Being a slave was no fun at all. Joseph had to do whatever he was told to do. And if he didn't, he would be beaten with a whip. But Joseph loved God, and he knew that God would be proud of him if he worked hard and made his master, Potiphar, happy.

"You are the best worker I have," Potiphar told Joseph. "I am going to put you in charge of my whole house."

Joseph did his best work for Potiphar. But one day Mrs. Potiphar told her husband a big lie about Joseph. And Potiphar threw Joseph in jail.

Being in jail was no fun at all. But Joseph loved God, and he knew that God would be proud of him if he were a happy and helpful prisoner.

Joseph was such a good prisoner that before long the jailer said, "I am going to put you in charge of all the other prisoners."

One day two of the prisoners told Joseph about their strange dreams. "There is no one here to tell us what they mean," the men said.

"God can tell you what your dreams mean," Joseph answered.

So the first man, who used to serve the king his drink, told Joseph his dream.

"That dream means that in three days the king will take you out of prison and give you your old job back," Joseph told him. Then the second man, who used to bake the king's bread, told Joseph his dream.

"That dream means that in three days you will lose your life," Joseph told him sadly.

Everything happened just as Joseph had said because God had given him understanding of what the two dreams meant.

—Linda Porter Carlyle

FROM PRISON TO PALACE

The magicians of Egypt stood shaking before the throne of the mighty pharaoh. He thundered at them, "What do you get paid for if you cannot tell me the meaning of my dreams?"

"Perhaps if *hem-ef* [his majesty] would be s-s-so kind as to t-t-tell us the dream once more?" one magician stammered.

"I dreamed I was standing by the mighty River Nile, giver of life. Seven fat cows, cooling themselves in the water, suddenly waded to shore and began feeding on the reeds. Then seven skinny cows, their ribs showing and hipbones sticking out like sails on a ship, followed the fat cows and ate them! But they stayed as thin as before.

"And I had another dream. I saw seven heads of ripe grain. Then seven other heads of grain, pale, withered, and drooping under the desert wind, swallowed the ripe and healthy grain.

"Who can tell me what these things mean?"

Completely baffled, the magicians could only stare at the pharaoh.

Just then the pharaoh's wine steward, the same one who had promised two years earlier to say a good word for Joseph, stepped forward. "Your Majesty," he quavered, "I remember something I promised to do. But I had forgotten about it."[1] Quickly he told

the king about Joseph.

"Send for him!" the king bellowed.

The sound of footsteps startled Joseph. Looking up, he saw a prison guard striding toward him. "Get up!" the guard snapped even before he had reached Joseph. "The king demands your presence! Immediately! Here's a change of clothes. When you've finished dressing, get a shave!" The guard looked down his nose at Joseph's beard, grown long during his prison stay. In Egypt only ignorant foreigners wore beards!

Within minutes Joseph found himself in the palace. And on the throne sat the pharaoh, his eyes mere slits as they bored suspiciously into Joseph.

Joseph bowed, but he hardly had time to stand up straight before the pharaoh challenged him. "I have had a dream. But no one can explain its meaning to me. I have heard that you can explain a dream when someone tells it to you."[2]

Archaelogists have uncovered many razors from ancient Egypt. Razors were used to shave boys' heads, leaving a long braid dangling by one cheek, and to keep men clean shaven.

"I am not able to explain the meaning of dreams," Joseph answered quickly.

For just an instant the king wondered, *Why should I trust this Hebrew slave who serves a God unknown to Egypt?*

But Joseph added quickly, "God will do this for *hem-ef.*"[3]

GENESIS 41:1-42:9

Two years later the king had a dream. . . . He saw seven fat . . . cows come up out of the river. . . . Then seven more cows came up. . . . But they were thin. . . . The seven thin . . . cows ate the seven . . . fat cows.

Then the king woke up. The king slept again and dreamed a second time. . . . He saw seven full . . . heads of grain. . . . After that, seven more heads of grain sprang up. But they were thin. . . . The thin heads of grain ate the seven full . . . heads. Then the king woke up again. . . . [The king] sent for all

the . . . wise men of Egypt. . . . But no one could explain their meaning. . . . Then the chief officer who served wine to the king said to him, "I remember something I promised to do. There was a time you were angry with me and the baker. You put us in prison. . . . We each had a dream. . . . A young

"In my dream I was standing on the bank of the Nile River,"[4] the pharaoh began, and he told Joseph all about the cows and the grain.

"Both of these dreams mean the same thing," Joseph answered promptly.[5]

Pharaoh leaned forward to hear Joseph more clearly. Joseph seemed so sure of what he was saying. "The seven good cows stand for seven years. And the seven good heads of grain stand for seven years," Joseph explained.[6] As he continued, Joseph identified the seven thin cows and the seven wilted heads of grain as seven years also.

Joseph paused, to let the king think briefly. Then Joseph continued, "You will have seven years of good crops and plenty to eat in all the land of Egypt. But after those seven years, there will come seven years of hunger. . . . The time of hunger will eat up the land. People will forget what it was like to have plenty of food."[7]

JOSEPH IS PROMOTED

The pharaoh could have had Joseph killed at any time. But the king was listening very carefully. So Joseph offered some advice. "Let *hem-ef* the king choose a man who is very wise and understanding. Let the king set him over the land of Egypt. And let the king also appoint officers over the land. They should take one-fifth of all the food that is grown during the seven good years. . . . They should store the grain in the cities and guard it. That food should be saved for later. It will be used during the seven years of hunger. . . . Then the people in Egypt will not die during the seven years of hunger."[8]

The king listened, wide-eyed, struck with the wisdom of Joseph's words. After a hurried conference with his advisors, he turned back to Joseph. "There is no one as wise and understanding as you are. . . . I put you in charge of all the land of Egypt."[9] And the pharaoh put his signet ring with the royal seal on Joseph's finger and gave him expensive new clothes to wear. He also gave Joseph an Egyptian name—Zaphenath-Paneah—and a wife, named Asenath.

Joseph, now 30 years old and vizier of Egypt, traveled all over the land, overseeing the building of storehouses for grain and organizing workers to take part of each harvest for the government. He kept careful records, but toward the end of seven years of unequaled harvest, he finally stopped weighing the grain, so plentiful it was like the sand of the sea.

Back in Canaan the rain had stopped and the land dried up, turning to dust. Jacob, his beard and hair pure white, gathered his sons together. "I have

> "THERE IS NO ONE AS WISE AND UNDERSTANDING AS YOU ARE. . . . I PUT YOU IN CHARGE OF ALL THE LAND OF EGYPT." AND THE PHAROAH PUT HIS SIGNET RING ON JOSEPH'S FINGER.

Hebrew man . . . explained their meanings. . . . Things happened exactly as he said. . . ."

So the king called for Joseph. . . .

The king said . . . , "I have had a dream, but no one can explain its meaning. . . . I have heard that you can explain a dream. . . ."

Joseph answered . . . , "I am not able to explain the meaning of dreams. God will do this for the king." . . .

"Both of these dreams mean the same thing." . . .

Jacob learned that there was grain in Egypt. So he said to his sons, ". . . Go down there and buy grain. . . . Then we will live and not die."

So ten of Joseph's brothers went down to buy grain from Egypt. . . .

Now Joseph was governor over Egypt. . . . Joseph's brothers came to him. They bowed facedown on the ground. . . .

Joseph knew they were his brothers.

Pharaoh made Joseph vizier (Egyptian: *tjaty*), "Superintendent of All Works of the King." The vizier oversaw nearly all aspects of government, including collection of taxes, monitoring the height of Nile flooding, and collecting grain into storehouses.

heard," he said, "that there is grain in Egypt. Go down there and buy grain for us to eat."[10]

One day as Joseph looked over a group of people appearing before him to ask for grain, his heart suddenly pounded and his hands shook. His brothers!

What should he do? To himself he said, *Are they sorry for what they did to me? Are they now treating Benjamin the way they used to treat me? Why isn't Benjamin with them?*

Joseph's brothers did not recognize this man called Zaphenath-Paneah as their brother. They bowed deeply. Joseph, looking down on them, suddenly remembered his dreams of grain and stars

bowing to him. He struggled to keep his face from showing his feelings. In a harsh voice he asked in the Egyptian language, "Where do you come from?"

"We have come from the land of Canaan to buy food."[11]

"You are spies!" he said with a frown.

Judah's face went white. The penalty for spying was slavery or death. "No, my master. We come as your servants just to buy food."[11]

Joseph leaned forward, eager to learn more, but fearful of what he might learn. "No! You have come to learn where this nation is weak!"

"Not so, sir," the brothers protested. "We are 10

of 12 brothers. We live in the land of Canaan. Our youngest brother is there with our father right now. And our other brother is gone." [12]

His father was still alive! Joseph caught his breath. They even referred to him, their brother Joseph. But Zaphenath-Paneah repeated, "I can see I was right! You are spies! But I will give you a way to prove you are telling the truth. . . . You will not leave this place until your youngest brother comes here. One of you must go and get your brother. The rest of you will stay here in prison. We will see if you are telling the truth." Then Zaphenath-Paneah ordered, "Guard! Throw these men in prison!" [13]

After three days the brothers were released from prison and standing once more before the dreaded prime minister.

FAMINES

The ancient Near East suffered from two kinds of famine.

Famine Resulting From Climatic Conditions—People in Palestine were always a rainfall or two away from famine—and death by starvation. Palestine had and still has one rainy season divided into two periods rain on either side of the rainy season.

Egypt, however, gets little rainfall and so depends on the 4,000-mile-long Nile River for irrigation. Each summer the Nile overflows. This flooding waters the land and adds a layer of fertile soil.

Rarely do both Palestine and Egypt suffer from drought conditions at the same time. But during the time of Joseph famine wracked both Palestine and Egypt.

In Old Testament times, between 2250 and 1950 B.C. the water level of the Nile was low, and a number of famines accompanied the drought. Also from 1200 to 900 B.C. famines broke out in Egypt, Mesopotamia, and Israel.

Sometimes the disaster of a famine from drought was made worse by accompanying disease (such as plague) and insects (such as locusts).

Famine Resulting From Sociological Conditions—Some famines resulted from political destabilization or from warfare. The ancient Hittite, Egyptian, and Assyrian armies would destroy gardens, cut down groves, and lay siege to a city so that it could not be resupplied with food. The result was a manufactured famine.

An ancient description of Pharaoh Thutmose III's military invasions said that in his thirtieth year he arrived at Kadesh, in Palestine, "destroying it. Felling its trees. Cutting down its grain" (*Ancient Near Eastern Texts*, p. 239). It took him seven months to starve the town of Megiddo into surrender.

Sometimes people got so desperate for food that they would try to eat leather, and fights would break out—even among family members—over a scrap of food. And, believe it or not, on occasion people turned to cannibalism to satisfy their hunger!

WILSON McCORD, 2001

During plagues, desert locusts have been known to swarm over more than 20 percent of the total land surface of the world.

"I am a God-fearing man. Do this thing, and I will let you live: If you are honest men, let one of your brothers stay here in prison. The rest of you go and carry grain back to feed your hungry families. Then bring your youngest brother back here to me." [14]

The 10 brothers talked hurriedly among themselves, not realizing that Zaphenath-Paneah could understand every word they said. "We are being punished for what we did to our brother [Joseph]. . . . That is why we are in this trouble now."[15] The guilt the brothers had suffered all through the years revealed itself in their words.

Then Reuben scolded his brothers. "I told you not to harm the boy. But you refused to listen to me."[16]

Joseph rushed from the room so his brothers wouldn't see the tears he could no longer hold back.

When he returned, he pointed to Simeon. "Put this one in prison," he directed. "Sell grain to the others and let them go home."

THE BIG SURPRISE

Jacob's sons spoke little as they traveled back toward Canaan. Just before nightfall they made camp. One of the brothers, preparing to feed his donkey, opened his grain sack. "The money I paid for the grain has been put back. Here it is in my sack!" he said.[17]

The money used by Jacob's sons was silver lumps. Coins were invented 1,100 years later, and paper money was invented in China nearly 2,000 years after that.

When the brothers reached Canaan, they told their father about the whole frightening experience. Jacob just stared at his sons. But another shock followed as all the men opened their sacks. In the top of each sack rested the silver they had paid for the grain! Bewildered and frightened, the brothers never imagined that the scheming vizier had returned their money.

Jacob grew very upset when they told him that Benjamin must accompany them on their next trip to Egypt. "You are robbing me of all my children," he cried. "Joseph is gone. Simeon is gone. And now you want to take Benjamin away, too."[18]

Reuben replied, "You may put my 2 sons to death if I don't bring Benjamin back to you. Trust him to my care."[19]

But nothing could convince Jacob to let Rachel's youngest son, grown dearer since Joseph had gone, go to Egypt, where a monstrous vizier waited to toy with the lives of his sons.

"I will not allow Benjamin to go."[20]

---

[1] Genesis 41:9, ICB.
[2] Verse 15, ICB.
[3] Verse 16, ICB.
[4] Verse 17, ICB.
[5] Verse 25, ICB.
[6] Verse 26, ICB.
[7] Verses 29-31, ICB.
[8] Verses 33-36, ICB.
[9] Verses 39-41, ICB.
[10] Genesis 42:2, ICB.
[11] Verses 7-10, ICB.
[12] Verses 12, 13, ICB.
[13] Verses 14-16, ICB.
[14] Verses 18-20, ICB.
[15] Verses 21, 22, ICB.
[16] Verse 22, ICB.
[17] Verse 28, ICB.
[18] Verse 36, ICB.
[19] Verse 37, ICB.
[20] Verse 38, ICB.

From Prison to Palace

"I had a dream last night," the king told his wise men. "I want you to tell me what it means."

The wise men nodded their heads. They listened carefully.

"I dreamed that seven fat, healthy cows came out of the Nile River," Pharaoh began. "Then seven ugly, skinny cows came out of the river. They ate up the fat cows."

The wise men shook their heads. They could not tell the king what his dream meant.

Then the man who served the king at his dinner table remembered something important. "When I was in prison," he said, "Joseph told me what my dream meant."

So the king sent for Joseph. "I heard that you can tell what dreams mean," he said.

"No," Joseph answered, "I can't. But God can."

The king told Joseph his dream about the seven skinny cows eating up the seven fat cows.

"God is telling you what He is going to do," Joseph said. "There will be seven years of plenty to eat with extra left over. And then there will be seven years of starving.

"Pick a wise man," Joseph went on, "and let him help the people save up food during the seven good years so that they will have something to eat in the seven bad years when no food grows. Then your people will not starve to death."

The king liked this idea. "Because God told you these things, you are the wisest man. I pick you. You will be in charge of everything." Then the king put his own special ring on Joseph's finger so that everybody would know Joseph was in charge.

That morning Joseph woke up as a prisoner. That night Joseph went to bed as the second most important ruler in all Egypt! And God was going to use Joseph to save many people's lives.

—LINDA PORTER CARLYLE

ONCE MORE TO EGYPT

Judah shook the grain sack again and again. Then he stared in dismay at the few kernels of wheat that fell to the bottom of the basket.

Benjamin, his eyes round with worry, stepped up behind Judah and gazed first at the nearly empty basket, and next at the few remaining sacks of grain. "How much longer can you put off going to Egypt for more grain?" Benjamin asked.

"I don't know," Judah answered, "but the cruel vizier insisted that you come with us next time and—"

"No!" The word sounded like the crack of a whip, cutting off Judah's words in mid-sentence.

Then Judah noticed Jacob standing nearby. "It's time," Jacob said. "Go to Egypt again. Buy a little more grain for us to eat."[1]

"The governor of that country strongly warned us. He said, 'Bring your brother back with you. If you don't, you will not be allowed to see me,'" Judah reminded his father.[2] And one by one the brothers described their starving animals, their hungry children, the dwindling supplies of grain.

Jacob's dark eyes blazed as he looked at his sons. "Why did you tell the man you had another brother?" he demanded. "You have caused me a lot of trouble."[3]

"But Father!" his sons exploded. "He questioned us carefully about ourselves and our family. . . . How could we know he would ask us to bring our other brother to him?"[4]

Jacob knew he must give in—or they'd starve to death, including Benjamin.

"Father," Judah spoke kindly but firmly, "send Benjamin with me. . . . I will guarantee you that he will be safe. . . . If I don't bring him back to you, you can blame me all my life."[5]

"If it has to be that way, then do this: Take some of the best foods in our land in your packs. Give them to the man as a gift. . . . Take twice as much money with you this time." Next his voice caught, and he just managed to whisper the words: "And take Benjamin with you. Now leave and go to the man."[6]

The brothers loaded their donkeys with presents and headed for faraway Egypt.

Joseph stood on the flat roof of his house overlooking the city.

Suddenly he spotted a dusty little caravan. As the donkeys and men came closer, he recognized his brothers! Hastily he counted. One, two, three . . . 10 in all! That meant Benjamin was with them! At least his brothers had not killed his little brother.

Joseph said to himself, *I have to know how they treat Benjamin. Are they teasing and bullying him the way they did me?*

Abruptly he strode to the door. "Sep!" he called,

As *tjaty* (vizier) it was Zaphenath-Paneah's (Joseph) responsibility to mobilize the Egyptian army, thereby making war on Jacob's clan in Canaan.

GENESIS 43:2–44:15

Jacob's family had eaten all the grain they had brought from Egypt. So Jacob said to them, "Go to Egypt again. Buy a little more grain for us to eat."

But Judah said to Jacob, "The governor of that country strongly warned us. . . . 'If you don't [bring your brother back with you], you will not be allowed to see me.' If you will send Benjamin with us, we will . . . buy food for you." . . .

Jacob said to them, ". . . Take Benjamin with you. Now leave and go to the man." . . .

In Egypt Joseph saw Benjamin with them. Joseph said to the servant in charge of his house, "Bring those men into my house. . . . Those men will eat with me today at noon." . . .

The brothers were afraid when they were brought to Joseph's house. . . . They bowed and a servant came hurrying. "This is what I want you to do . . ."

Fearfully Jacob's sons approached the servant who had run out to meet them. Would he arrest them for thievery?

"Sir," they explained, "we came here once before to buy food. While we were going home, we stopped for the night and opened our sacks. Each of us found all his money in his sack. We brought that money with us to give it back to you. . . . We don't know who put that money in our sacks."

"Don't be afraid," the servant said, shrugging. "Your God . . . must have put the money in your sacks. I got the money you paid me for the grain last time."[7]

The brothers stared at one another. Somehow they feared kindness from this strange vizier of Egypt more than they feared his harsh, stern words.

THE BANQUET

Soon the servant brought Simeon from prison so he could join them, and the servant told the 11 men to follow him. Clutching their gifts, they almost tip-toed behind the servant as he led them to Zaphenath-Paneah's beautiful home. As they sat down in their dusty robes, the servant brought water and washed their feet. No one said anything as he stared at the others, wondering what would happen next!

At noon they were ushered into a large dining room with tables and stools, but the brothers noticed only one thing—the prime minister! Bowing before him like sheaves of grain in the wind, the brothers

As much as 60 percent of a farmer's crop was confiscated by the acient *tjaty* (vizier) and put into government granaries.

again did not recognize that this stately Zaphenath-Paneah was really their brother Joseph.

"Arise," he ordered, being careful not to look at Benjamin. "How is your health?"

In quavering voices the brothers answered that they were well.

"How is your aged father you told me about? Is he still alive?" he asked, trying hard to keep the eagerness from his voice.

"Your servant, our father, is well."

Joseph could no longer keep his eyes off Benjamin—his own little brother standing before him after all these years! He took note of his thin cheeks, a sure sign of the widespread famine. "God be good to you, my son!" he said, and suddenly he ran from the room, crying silently.[8]

---

low . . . to show him respect. . . . [Joseph] said, "Serve the meal." . . .

Then Joseph gave a command to the servant in charge of his house. He said, ". . . Put my silver cup in the sack of the youngest brother. Also put his money for the grain in that sack." The servant did what Joseph told him. . . . They were not far from the city when Joseph said to the servant . . . , "Go after the men." . . .

The servant said, ". . . The man who has taken the cup will become my slave. The rest of you may go free."

Then every brother quickly lowered his sack to the ground and opened it. The servant searched the sacks. . . . He found the cup in Benjamin's sack. The brothers tore their clothes to show they were sad. Then they put their sacks back on the donkeys. And they returned to the city.

At last Joseph returned and, with a wave of his hand, directed the servants to serve dinner.

The brothers found themselves seated around a large table, while the vizier sat by himself at another. Palm fronds, to keep the flies away, lay within easy reach.

Suddenly, puzzled looks crossed the brothers' faces. Reuben, the oldest, sat at the head of their table. Next to him sat Simeon, then Levi, then all the other brothers in order of their ages. Last came Benjamin, the youngest. How does he know our ages? the brothers wondered to themselves.

But they had little time to wonder, for the servants were bringing the food. The brothers stared as mounds of meat, heaps of vegetables, stacks of melon, baskets of bread, piles of pastries, and jugs of wine appeared. But for every piece of meat or dainty pastry the servants gave the brothers, they gave Benjamin five times as much.

From his separate table Zaphenath-Paneah watched carefully. How would the men react as they saw Benjamin favored? Would their old jealousy spring up? Would they mutter under their breaths, complaining that Benjamin had five times as much food as they?

But Reuben and Issachar and Gad and even Simeon smiled as they watched Benjamin enjoying the feast. The other brothers laughed softly as Benjamin's pale, thin cheeks bulged with great mouthfuls of food.

At the end of the meal the brothers felt relaxed—and full! They still did not understand this strange vizier, but he had treated them like important guests.

Joseph—or Zaphenath-Paneah—almost believed that his cruel brothers had changed, but he decided to test them once more. Calling his servants, he instructed them, "Fill the men's sacks

with as much grain as they can carry. And put each man's money into his sack with the grain. Put my silver cup in the sack of the youngest brother."[9]

The next morning the brothers arose with the sun and, humming happily, loaded their donkeys with bulging sacks of grain. How pleased Jacob would be to see them return, loaded with food, and with Benjamin well and unhurt!

Just outside the city, the brothers looked back in surprise as they heard the sound of hoofbeats and chariot wheels. Zaphenath-Paneah's servant pulled up to a stop. Jumping from their chariots, he shouted, "Why have you paid back evil for good? The cup you have stolen is the one my master uses for drinking. . . . You have done a very wicked thing!"[10]

"St-t-tolen a cup?" they stammered, too surprised even to think clearly.

"Yes!" the servant answered.

The brothers found words. "If you find that silver cup in the sack of one of us, then let him die. And we will be your slaves."

"We will do as you say. But only the man who has taken the cup will become my slave. The rest of you may go free," the servant answered.[11]

Each brother pulled the grain sacks off the backs of the patient donkeys. The servant began opening each sack.

When he opened Benjamin's sack, the brothers' hearts nearly stopped, for there, nestled in the grain, rested Zaphenath-Paneah's silver goblet!

Feeling as if they moved in a nightmare, the brothers reloaded their donkeys and headed once more toward the palace and the wrath of the vizier.

---

[1] Genesis 43:2, ICB.
[2] Verse 3, ICB.
[3] Verse 6, ICB.
[4] Verse 7, ICB.
[5] Verses 8, 9, ICB.
[6] Verses 11-13, ICB.
[7] Verses 20-23, ICB.
[8] Verses 27-29, ICB.
[9] Genesis 44:1, 2, ICB.
[10] Verses 4, 5, ICB.
[11] Verses 9, 10, ICB.

Divining cups were used throughout the ancient Near East. Through the reflected patterns of the water in the cup (sometimes gems or molten wax were dropped in) the diviner claimed to learn the will of the gods.

Once More to Egypt

apa Jacob's stomach rumbled. He was hungry, but there was not enough food to eat. "I have heard that there is food in Egypt," he said to his sons. "Go, buy some for us!"

So the brothers traveled the long, long way to Egypt. When they got there, they went to the man in charge of selling food. The man in charge was Joseph, their little brother! But they did not recognize him.

When Joseph saw his brothers bowing down before him, he remembered his dreams of long ago.

Joseph did not tell his brothers who he was, but he asked them about their family back home. He found out that his precious papa was still alive! And his little brother Benjamin was home with him. "The next time you come back to buy food, be sure to bring your littlest brother with you." Joseph ordered.

"Never!" Papa Jacob hollered when the brothers returned home with the food. "Never! Benjamin may not go to Egypt with you!"

But when the family ran out of food again, Papa Jacob had to change his mind and let Benjamin go.

Joseph was so happy to see his brothers again—especially Benjamin! But he wanted to know if the older brothers were nicer than they had been. Did they hate Benjamin the same way they used to hate him?

Joseph decided to test them. He hid his special cup in one of Benjamin's sacks.

"Stop!" called the guard as the brothers were leaving town.

"You stole the silver cup of the man in charge!"

"We did not!" the brothers said.

"Whoever stole the cup will stay here and be a slave!" the guard shouted. And when he looked, the guard found Joseph's special silver cup in a sack on Benjamin's donkey.

The brothers couldn't believe it. If they didn't take Benjamin home with them, Papa Jacob would die of sadness. The brothers followed the guard back to Joseph's palace.

—LINDA PORTER CARLYLE

TOGETHER AGAIN!

Once again the 11 sons of Jacob bowed themselves to the floor before Zaphenath-Paneah. Their hearts hammered in their chests, and they trembled with fear.

His lips pressed together in a thin, angry line, the Egyptian vizier coldly stared at the men. "What have you done? Didn't you know that a man like me can learn things by signs and dreams?"[1]

Judah struggled to his feet. "Sir, what can we say? And how can we show we are not guilty? God has uncovered our guilt."[2] At those words Joseph's brothers remembered the cruel, unspeakable crime they had committed against Joseph. They never dreamed, of course, it was he standing right before them—that Zaphenath-Paneah was really Joseph!

Judah continued: "So all of us will be your slaves, not just Benjamin."[3]

Smoothly Joseph replied, "I will not make you all slaves! Only the man who stole the cup will be my slave." Will they choose to leave Benjamin here as a slave, not caring what happens to him or that my father will grieve? Joseph wondered. "The rest of you may go back safely to your father," he concluded and turned to leave.[4]

"Sir, please let me speak plainly to you," Judah pleaded, moving closer to Joseph. "Please don't be angry with me. I know that you are as powerful as the king of Egypt himself."[5]

Judah paused, clearing his throat, and then continued: "When we were here before, you asked us, 'Do you have a father or a brother?' And we answered you, 'We have an old father. And we have a younger brother. . . . This youngest son's brother is dead. So he is the only one of his mother's children left alive. And our father loves him very much." [6]

Again Judah stopped briefly, letting the translator put his words into the Egyptian language, for he didn't know that the vizier could understand the Canaanite language. "Then you said to us, 'Bring that brother to me. I want to see him.'" [7] Judah hoped that his words were convincing this stern Egyptian to treat them kindly. "I gave my father a guarantee that the young boy would be safe. I said to my father, 'If I don't bring him back to you, you can blame me

Joseph greets Benjamin, his younger brother. Rachel, while dying in giving birth, named him Ben-Oni, "Son of My Sorrow/Pain." Jacob renamed the baby Benjamin, "Son of [the] South/Right Hand," which probably meant "Lucky."

all my life.' So now, please allow me to stay here and be your slave. And let the young boy go back home with his brothers. I cannot go back to my

---

GENESIS 44:14–45:15

When Judah and his brothers went back to Joseph's house, Joseph was still there. The brothers bowed facedown on the ground before him. Joseph said to them, "What have you done? Didn't you know that a man like me can learn things by signs and dreams?" . . .

"The man who stole the cup will be my slave. The rest of you may go back safely to your father." . . .

Then Judah went to Joseph and said, "Sir, please let me speak plainly to you. . . . I gave my father a guarantee that the young boy would be safe. . . . So now, please allow me to stay here and be your slave. And let the young boy go back home with his brothers." . . .

Joseph could not control himself in front of his servants any longer. He cried out, father if the boy is not with me. I couldn't stand to see my father that sad." [8]

Joseph stood like a statue during Judah's plea. Only a tiny muscle twitched in his smooth face, but he felt his heart would burst. He had his answer! The love in Judah's words, the silent plea in the eyes of his other brothers, proved that the evil men who had plotted murder and sold their own brother as a slave had changed.

With a sudden cry Joseph commanded his servants and the interpreter to leave the room. Instantly the 11 men felt a pang of terror. What was Zaphenath-Paneah going to do to them when there were no witnesses?

Then, facing his brothers, with tears running down his cheeks, Zaphenath-Paneah proclaimed in their own Canaanite language, "I am Joseph. Is my father still alive?" [9]

But the brothers heard only the words "I am Joseph!" They stood as if struck by lightning, the words roaring in their ears. How could this vizier of the most powerful land on earth be Joseph? And, oh, if it was he, what dreadful thing would

REVIEW AND HERALD PHOTO DATABASE

Pharaoh gave Joseph his signet ring. Such rings contained the king's names and titles. Using it to seal documents and other objects guaranteed authenticity.

he do to them to get even for their terrible deed?

But Joseph stood with his arms outstretched. "Come close to me." [10]

The 11 men slinked closer to this strange man who did not look anything like the Joseph they had sold.

"I am your brother Joseph," he repeated. His 11 brothers still wondered if it could be true. Joseph continued, "Now don't be worried. Don't be angry with yourselves because you sold me there. No food has grown on the land for two years now. And there will be five more years without planting or harvest. So God sent me here ahead of you. . . . It was to keep you alive in an amazing way." [11]

Slowly recognition dawned on Joseph's brothers. They remembered the dreams of that 17-year-old boy, dreams they had determined would never come true. Yet here they were, bowing before him, depending on him for their very lives.

Joseph had not finished, though. "God has made me the highest officer of the king of Egypt. I am in charge of his palace. . . . So leave quickly and go to my father. Tell him, 'Your son Joseph says: God has

"Have everyone leave me." . . . Only the brothers were left with Joseph. . . . He said to his brothers, "I am Joseph." . . . The brothers could not answer him, because they were very afraid of him.

So Joseph said to them, "Come close to me." . . . "Don't be worried. Don't be angry with yourselves because you sold me here. God sent me here ahead of you to save people's lives. . . . Go to my father. Tell him, 'Your son Joseph says: . . . Come down to me quickly. Live in the land of Goshen. You will be near me. . . . I will care for you. . . . You and your family . . . will not starve.' . . . Tell

my father about how powerful I have become in Egypt. . . . Hurry and bring him back to me." . . .

Then Joseph kissed all his brothers. He cried as he hugged them. After this, his brothers talked with him.

Joseph sent to his father 10 male donkeys loaded with the best Egyptian products and 10 female donkeys bearing various kinds of food. Pharaoh provided horse-drawn (or cattle-drawn) two-wheeled carts for the women and children to ride in during the return trip to Egypt. The clothing Joseph gave to his brothers may have been festal garments, comparable to our formal wear.

made me master over all Egypt. Come down to me quickly. Live in the land of Goshen. You will be near me. . . . I will care for you during the next five years of hunger.' "[12]

Then Joseph flung his arms around Benjamin, and the two brothers, who had not seen each other for more than 20 years, clung to each other. One by one Joseph hugged and kissed all his brothers, and they all laughed . . . and cried . . . and wiped tears from their eyes . . . and then cried some more.

Until far into the night Jacob's 12 sons, together again, talked and talked, trying hard to catch up on all that had happened since they had last seen each other.

Soon word reached Pharaoh that Zaphenath-Paneah's brothers had come to Egypt! The whole palace buzzed with the news. Everyone knew that Zaphenath-Paneah had been a slave, but until now no one had known that he was the son of a respected nomad in the land of Canaan. The pharaoh was delighted.

Words tumbled from the king's lips as he said to Zaphenath-Paneah, "Tell your brothers to load their animals and go back to the land of Canaan. Tell them to bring their father and their families back here to me. I will give them the best land in Egypt. And they will eat the best food we have here. Tell them to take some wagons from Egypt for their children and their wives. And tell them to bring there father back also. Tell them not to worry about bringing any of their things with them. We will give them the best of what we have in Egypt."[13]

Joseph smiled, glad that the king agreed with his plan!

SURPRISE FOR JACOB

As the brothers prepared to go back to Canaan, Joseph handed each of them a brand-new robe. But to Benjamin he gave five new robes, as well as seven and a half pounds of silver! And all the brothers smiled happily at Benjamin, without a trace of jealousy.

To his father Joseph sent 10 donkeys loaded down with all kinds of good things from Egypt, and then 10 more donkeys loaded down with food to keep everyone from getting hungry on the trip back to Egypt.

Joseph waved and waved as his brothers' caravan disappeared in the dust. And he shouted after them, "Don't quarrel on the way home." He could hardly wait until that caravan returned with his father! After all these years he would be reunited with his whole family.

Jacob sat dozing in the sun, dreaming of those long-ago days when little Joseph tagged barefoot at his heels, while Rachel smiled from the opening of the tent. Suddenly he heard the braying of donkeys and loud, excited voices.

He sprang to his feet as fast as his old bones and lame hip would let him. His sons, mounted on donkeys, pulled up before him. Many other donkeys, some laden with bulging sacks, others pulling wagons such as Jacob had never seen before, trailed his sons.

Jacob's daughters-in-law and grandchildren and servants came running from all directions. *Food! Food*

Notice the Canaan dog in the picture. This reconstructed breed dates back to biblical times. They make good pets and guard dogs.

from Egypt, was their only thought, but Jacob's sons had a surprise for them much better than food.

"Father," they spoke gently, when the excitement had died down a bit, "we have some news for you, and we think you'd better sit down."

"What is it?" Jacob asked curiously. His first thought upon his sons' arrival had been to look for Benjamin, and Benjamin stood before him—alive. And Simeon had returned. Food, more food than he had imagined his sons might bring, overflowed from the donkeys' backs. What news could there be?

Carefully, slowly, the brothers spoke. "Father, Joseph is alive, and he is the vizier of Egypt!"

Jacob's heart went numb. What cruel joke was this his sons were playing on him? *Joseph, oh, Joseph!* he thought. *If only it were true!*

Patiently his 12 sons explained all that had happened. "Look at the wagons, Father—Joseph sent them. Look at the clothes, at Benjamin's silver—Joseph gave them to him. Look at all the extra food and animals—Joseph sent them to you because he wants us to move to Egypt and live near him. He especially wants to see you, Father—Joseph does."

Suddenly Jacob felt better than he had for many years. "My son Joseph is still alive," he said. "I will go and see him before I die." [14]

[1] Genesis 44:15, ICB.
[2] Verse 16, ICB.
[3] Verse 16, ICB.
[4] Verse 17, ICB.
[5] Verse 18, ICB.
[6] Verses 19, 20, ICB.
[7] Verse 21, ICB.
[8] Verses 32-34, ICB.
[9] Genesis 45:3, ICB.
[10] Verse 4, ICB.
[11] Verses 4-7, ICB.
[12] Verses 8-11, ICB.
[13] Verses 17-20, ICB.
[14] Verse 28, ICB.

Together Again!

When the brothers got back to Joseph's palace, they fell down on the ground before him.

"The man who stole my cup will be my slave!" Joseph shouted.

"Please listen to me," Judah begged. "I promised our father I would take care of our youngest brother. If we go home without him, our father will die of sadness. Please let me take Benjamin's place. I will stay here and be your slave! Let Benjamin go home to our father," he begged.

Then Joseph knew that his brothers had changed. They were not selfish and jealous anymore. Tears ran down his face. "I am your brother Joseph!" he cried.

The brothers could not believe what they had just been told!

"Don't be worried," Joseph said. "God wanted me here in Egypt so I could keep you and your families alive during these years that food will not grow. God made me the man in charge of selling food."

The brothers were still so surprised that they couldn't talk.

"Hurry home, and get my father!" Joseph ordered. "Bring him and all your families back here to Egypt. There will be five more years when food will not grow. I will take care of you." Joseph hugged and kissed each of his brothers. Joseph gave his brothers wagons for the trip. He gave them new clothes and money and plenty of food.

The brothers talked all the way home. "Joseph is alive!" "Think how happy Papa is going to be!" "How are we going to tell Papa what we did to Joseph?" "Can you believe that Joseph forgave us for what we did to him?" "God is using him to save our lives!"

—LINDA PORTER CARLYLE

- The great sphinx has a lion's body and a human head. It is 240 feet long and 66 feet high. Each paw is 56 feet long, and the head and face are 30 feet long and 14 feet wide.

- Pharaoh Khafre (Chephren) probably had the great sphinx constructed around 2500 B.C. It is the first sphinx ever made.

Originally the great sphinx had not only a beard but also a covering called a *nemes* headcloth. A uraeus cobra was on its forehead. The body and face were painted red, and the headdress was painted with blue and yellow stripes. (Traces of paint can still be seen.)

© PHOTODISC

• The Great Pyramid covers 13 acres. Originally it was 755.8 feet long on each of its three sides and 480.06 feet high. The angle of inclination for the sides is about 51.5 degrees. It contains (estimates vary) about 590,700 cut and dressed blocks.

• The volume of the rocks in the Great Pyramid is such that they could pave a highway eight feet wide and four inches thick stretching from New York City to San Francisco.

The Great Pyramid of Cheops (Khufu) was one of the Seven Wonders of the Ancient World and is the only wonder still in existence. It can be seen from the moon. The temperature inside is always 68 degrees Fahrenheit.

- Cairo is home for about 16 million people, twice as many people as live in New York City.

- The Nile River is 4,160 miles long, the longest river in the world.

- Cotton dishdashers are a common garment worn by men in Egypt. A similar robe for women is called a galabia.

The two men are playing the rebab, also called the Arab fiddle or a spike fiddle. It has two strings, though some have only one, while others may have three. Through the rebab the bow came to be used in Europe.

Even today Egyptians use camels and donkeys as beasts of burden.

The background photo is of the Tahrir bridge over the Nile River. The bridge connects Cairo and Gazira Island. The photo is taken from the Cairo Tower. In the background are several modern hotels, including the Ramses Hilton, the Helnan Shepheard, Semiramis Intercontinental, and Le Meridian hotels.

BIBLE GLOSSARY/DICTIONARY

Here is a list of the biblical people and places mentioned in this book. The glossary not only gives information about each person and place, but also provides two guides that use easy-to-understand pronunciation apparatus. When a syllable is given in all CAPITAL letters, that is the syllable you put the stress on.

The first pronunciation offered is how most people who speak American English say the name. The second pronunciation is truly special. It tells you how to pronounce the name in Hebrew, Egyptian, Persian, Babylonian, Aramaic, or Greek. You will now know how, for instance, Eli pronounced Samuel's name when he called him! We give special thanks to Leona G. Running, expert in ancient Near Eastern languages, for preparing the pronunciation guides.

Have fun reading about these fascinating people and places of long ago. And enjoy the edge you'll have when it comes to biblical trivia, because you will be able to pronounce those tongue-twisting names just as they were spoken in the ancient Near East.

ABRAHAM—*American English pronunciation: AY-bra-ham. Hebrew pronunciation: av-ra-HAHM.* The name meant "the father is exalted" and was a very old name that has been found in a number of ancient inscriptions, sometimes beginning with the letter "I" rather than "A." Born in Ur, Abram (right) lived in Haran until his father, Terah, died. Then God told him to leave for an unknown land—the "promised land"—Canaan. Although we cannot pinpoint with absolute accuracy the dates in Abraham's life, we shall assume that he was born in

Abraham

1950 B.C., which means he left Haran when he was 75 years old—in 1875 B.C. Abraham died at 175 years of age—in 1775 B.C. When Abraham was 100 years old, Isaac was born.

ASENATH—*American English pronunciation: ASS-e-nath. Hebrew pronunciation of the Egyptian word: ah-se-NATH.* Is a Hebrew transliteration of the Egyptian name Ns-Nìt or 'Iws-Nìt, both of which mean "the one belonging to (the goddess) Neith." Asenath was the daughter of Potiphera, who was a priest at Heliopolis (also known as On). Asenath gave birth to two sons, Manasseh and Ephraim, who became the ancestors of two Israelite tribes.

ASHER—*American English pronunciation: ASH-er. Hebrew pronunciation: ah-SHARE.* This proper name means "happy" or "happy one." Some scholars speculate that the name may also originally have been "Ashar," the name of a god in Amorite and Old Akkadian personal names. He was the son of Zilpah and Jacob—Jacob's eighth son.

Benjamin

His ancestors formed the Israelite tribe of Asher. Asherites lived in two distinct areas. The first was in Galilee and was a strip of land that extended to the Mediterranean Sea. This territory was especially suited for growing grapes and olives. The second was farther south in the southernmost part of the hill country of the Ephraimites. The territory was mentioned in Egyptian texts as early as the 1200s B.C. during the reign of Pharaoh Seti I and later during the reign of Rameses II.

BENJAMIN—*American English pronunciation: BEN-ja-min. Hebrew pronunciation: bin-yah-MEEN.* This male name meant "son of my right hand" in Hebrew. The Old Testament mentions four men by this name. In this book, Benjamin is Jacob's youngest son, who was born to Rachel during their trip from Bethel to Ephrath. Rachel died during the birth. Just before she died she named her baby Ben-oni, which means "son of my sorrow." Jacob renamed him Benjamin. Benjamin's

Dan

CANAAN—*American English pronunciation: KAY-nan. Hebrew pronunciation: ke-NA-ahn.* Canaan (sometimes spelled Chanaan) probably comes from a root word that describes the color reddish purple, which was a dye made in the area. In the Bible Canaan is the equivalent of Palestine—the area between the Mediterranean Sea and the Jordan River. The people who lived there are called Canaanites, and were descendants of Ham's son by the same name. Many Canaanites were traders or merchants. Although the Canaanites had Hamitic roots, the language they spoke was a Semitic variety, which the Israelites picked up when they moved into the Promised Land. The language later became known as Hebrew. Canaan was occupied long before the exodus from Egypt and the conquest of the land under Joshua. The Canaanites worshiped many gods and goddesses, among them: El, Baal, Anath, Asherah, Dagon, Mot, Yam, and Hadad. Their religion was basically a fertility cult, which for many hundreds of years appealed to both the Judahites and Israelites.

descendants constituted the tribe of Benjamin, from which King Saul, first king of the Israelite monarchy, came. King Saul expanded the territory of Benjamin. Many Benjaminites were left-handed and were known for their skill with a sling. Under the rule of Alexander the Great the territories of Benjamin and Judah were merged into the territory known as Youdaia.

BILHAH—*American English pronunciation: BIL-hah. Hebrew pronunciation:* *bil-HAH.* Bilhah (her name may mean "not worried") was a maidservant given to Rachel by Laban for a wedding present. When Rachel was unable to become pregnant, she asked Jacob to take Bilhah as a secondary wife. This was in harmony with an ancient Near Eastern custom at the time, which allowed a barren wife to give a slave girl to her husband. The child from that liaison would be the heir and was considered to be the son of the original wife. Bilhah give birth to Dan and Naphtali.

DAN—*American English pronunciation: DAN. Hebrew pronunciation: DAHN.* The Hebrew word means "judge." In the Old Testament Dan refers to a person, a tribe, and a town. In this book the man himself is featured. Dan was born to Jacob and Bilhah, Rachel's maidservant. His brother was Naphtali. Dan had one son—Hushim, who was also known as Shuham. The Bible tells us nothing about Dan's life and exploits. He was the ancestor of the small tribe of Dan, which inherited land on the west coast of Canaan, which was occupied by the Philistines. In the Sinai Wilderness, Oholiab, a descendant of Dan, helped Bezalel construct the Mosaic tabernacle. Samson, the strong man, belonged to the tribe of Dan.

DOTHAN—*American English pronunciation: DOE-than. Hebrew pronunciation: doh-THAHN.* Dothan was a Canaanite city situated along a trade route between the Plain of Esdraelon and Samaria. Today the area is known as Tell Dôthan, which is about 10 miles north of Samaria.

Dothan as a city existed from 3200 B.C. During the 2nd century B.C. a 13-foot wall was constructed to protect the city. The city covered about 25 acres. When Joseph found his brothers here with their flocks, they threw him in a dried up cistern and then sold him to a trading caravan that happened by. The traders, sometimes called Ishmaelites and sometimes called Midianites, took Joseph to Egypt and there sold him to Potiphar.

EGYPT—*American English pronunciation: EE-jipt. Hebrew pronunciation: mits-RAH-yim.* The present English word "Egypt" comes from the Greek. In the Old Testament Egypt was known as Misrayim. This northeastern African country was divided into Upper Egypt (the Nile Delta, also known as the "Black Land") and Lower Egypt (the Nile River Valley, also known as the "Red Land"). The Hebrew ending *im* is a dual ending, probably referring to this distinction. Although technically part of the Sahara Desert, Egypt has been a fertile land because of the Nile River, which overflows its banks each year, bringing irrigation and rich mud in

Cairo, Capital City of Egypt

the Nile River Delta. Wheat, barley, flax, and grapes have been the main crops for thousands of years. Also in areas date palms, fig trees, acacias, and sycamores thrive, but Egypt has never had any forests. In the swampy areas, papyrus grew in abundance, and the Egyptians used the plant to make what eventually came to be known as paper. Egypt also has had some interesting wild animals living in its territory—Nile crocodiles, hippopotami, hyenas, and jackals. The people who lived in ancient Egypt were Hamitic, not Semitic, descendants of Noah's son Ham. The earliest Egyptians appear to have been slight of stature with swarthy complexions and black hair. These farmers expanded their horizons, and ultimately Egypt became one of the great nations of the ancient world. The Egyptian kings were known as "pharaohs." The Egyptians worshiped many gods and became especially concerned about the journey to a better land for those who died, and so much effort was expended in building elaborate graves—especially the pyramids. Joseph ended up in Egypt as a slave and later as second to the pharaoh himself. Joseph moved his entire family to Egypt, where they lived for many years. Moses was born in Egypt and ultimately led the Israelites in the exodus from Egypt to the Promised Land.

GAD—*American English pronunciation: GAD. Hebrew pronunciation: GAD.* The name, which sometimes referred to a god, probably means "good fortune." Gad was Jacob's seventh son and was the son of Zilpah. His descendants constituted the tribe of Gad. There is varying scriptural evidence about exactly where the tribal territory was located. (A different man by the name of Gad is also mentioned in the Bible He was a seer during the time of King David.)

ISAAC—*American English pronunciation: EYE-zak. Hebrew pronunciation: yits-HAHKH.* The name Isaac means "he laughs." He was the second son of Abraham and Sarah, the child God promised through whom the whole world would be blessed. Abraham was 100 years old and Sarah 90 when

Isaac

Isaac was born. Isaac married Rebekah, and they had two sons—Jacob and Esau. He was 180 years old when he died.

ISHMAEL/ISHMAELITES

—American English pronunciation: ISH-ma-ell. Hebrew pronunciation: yish-mah-AYL. In the Bible we read of six different people bearing the name Ishmael. The person featured in this book was the person born to Abram and Sarai's Egyptian maidservant Hagar. The name means "God hears." Having an heir through a concubine or secondary wife was in keeping with ancient Mesopotamia law. Abram was 86 years old when Ishmael was born—11 years since he had entered the land of Canaan. When Ishmael was 13 years old, God told Abraham that the males in his household should be circumcised, and Abraham complied. One year later Isaac was born. A few years later, because Ishmael had been mocking Isaac, Abraham expelled Hagar and Ishmael (who was by now somewhere between 15 and 18 years old; we do not know exactly how old Isaac was when he was weaned, but he may have been at least 3 years

Ishmael

old). God miraculously provided water for them in the desert. Ishmael lived to be 137 years old. His descendants were called Ishmaelites.

ISSACHAR—*American English pronunciation: ISS-a-car. Hebrew pronunciation: yissah-KAHR.* This masculine name means "there is hire" or "man for hire." The Old Testament mentions two men with this name. The Issachar in this book is Jacob's ninth son and Leah's fifth son. The circumstances surrounding his birth are interesting—some

might say bizarre. Leah, who had given birth to several children, suddenly found herself barren—a condition that had plagued her sister Rachel, of whom Jacob was especially fond. When Leah's oldest son Reuben came home with some mandrakes that he had found, Rachel immediately asked for them. (Mandrakes were considered to enhance fertility.) Leah told Rachel that she could have the mandrakes on one condition—Leah would spend the night with Jacob. The deal was struck, Leah slept with Jacob, and soon Leah found herself pregnant with Issachar. Issachar was the ancestor of the Israelite tribe of Issachar. The Bible tells us very little about this man who had four sons. The royal city of Jezreel, where King Ahab and Queen Jezebel built a winter palace, was located in the territory allotted to the tribe of Issachar. Also several important battles took place within the territory of Issachar.

JACOB—*American English pronunciation: JAY-cob. Hebrew pronunciation: yah-a-KOHV.* The Bible mentions two men by the name of Jacob—one in the Old Testament and the other in the New Testament. The name means "heel grabber." The Jacob featured in this book is the Old Testament Jacob, son of Isaac and Rebekah and twin of Esau. Jacob, whose name was later changed to Israel, was the progenitor of the Hebrew (Israelite) people. Jacob, unlike his hunter brother, Esau, was a quiet person who enjoyed herding flocks. Rebekah favored Jacob, whereas Esau was Isaac's favorite son. Esau sold his birthright to Jacob for a meal of lentils, and later

Joseph

Jacob, under Rebekah's prodding, impersonated Esau when Isaac, who was blind and ill at age 137, wanted to give Esau what he felt was his final blessing before his [Issac's] death. Esau grew so enraged at Jacob's deceit that he threatened to murder him. Jacob, now 77 years old, fled to Haran in Mesopotamia, where he lived with Uncle Laban for 20 years. When Jacob, now Israel, returned to Canaan, he took up residence in Succoth, Shechem, and then Bethel. Jacob fathered 12 sons and one daughter, whose name was

Dinah. When he was 130 years old, Jacob moved to Egypt, where his long-lost son Joseph was vizier to the pharaoh during a time of severe famine. He lived in Egypt for 17 years and died at age 147. Jacob was later buried in the Cave of Machpelah, which Abraham had purchased when Sarah died.

JOSEPH—*American English pronunciation: JOE-zeff. Hebrew pronunciation: yoh-SAYF.* Fourteen different men in the Bible share the name

Joseph, which in Hebrew means "may he add." The Old Testament Joseph featured in this book was the son of Jacob and Rachel. Jacob was 91 years old when Joseph was born and had served Laban for 14 years—six years before the family moved back to Canaan. Jacob especially favored Joseph and made him a special garment that was the envy of Joseph's brothers. When Joseph began having dreams in which his brothers and other family members gave him great deference, the jealousy became even more vitriolic. When Jacob sent 17-year-old Joseph to find his brothers, who had taken the flocks to Shechem and then to Dothan, the brothers ripped off his coat, threw Joseph into a dry well, and ultimately sold him to Ishmaelite traders for 20 silver shekels. The brothers smeared blood over Joseph's coat and tore it so that Jacob would think Joseph had been attacked, killed, and eaten by a wild animal—perhaps a wolf or a lion. In Egypt Joseph was sold to Potiphar. Later accused of sexual assault by Potiphar's wife, Joseph ended up in prison. Thirteen years later he was released when he interpreted a dream for the pharaoh, who

then made Joseph second in command in Egypt. Joseph married Asenath, daughter of the Egyptian priest at Heliopolis (also called On). He and Asenath had two boys—Manasseh and Ephraim. Joseph gathered grain during seven years with bountiful harvest, and then dispersed the grain during seven years of devastating famine.

JUDAH—*American English pronunciation: JOO-dah. Hebrew pronunciation: ye-hoo-DAH.* The Old Testament mentions six men with the

name Judah, which may mean "let Him [God] be praised." The Judah mentioned in this book was Jacob's fourth son by Leah. Judah married Shua, a Canaanite girl, who bore him three sons. Judah is the one who, to save Joseph's life, suggested that the brothers sell him to the Ishmaelites. It was not a particularly good option, but at least Judah spared Joseph's life, and God saw to it that in turn Joseph, as vizier of Egypt, was later able to spare his family's life by providing them with food during the terrible famine that

Judah

Rachel

Naphtali's territory in the Promised Land was densely forested as well as being mountainous. The tribe of Naphtali tried to vanquish the towns of Beth-shemesh and Beth-anat but failed. Instead they subjected the citizens of those cities to forced labor. During the time of King Solomon, Hiram, king of Tyre, was said to have been born to a widow from Naphtali. When Assyrian King Tiglath-pileser invaded Palestine, he destroyed the tribe and carried off many prisoners of war from Naphtali.

POTIPHAR—*American English pronunciation: POT-eh-fer. Hebrew pronunciation: poh-tee-FAR.* This is a transliteration of an Egyptian name that means "the one whom the (sun-god) Ra has given." The full name was Poti-phera. In 1935 an inscription was found that bore this name, identifying the individual as an officer of the king and captain of the king's bodyguard. It is not likely that this is the same man who purchased Joseph, however. The Bible says that he was a eunuch, the implication of which is debated among scholars. Joseph was sold to Potiphar as a slave. Potiphar's

wracked both Egypt and Canaan, an unusual occurrence. Judah was the progenitor of the tribe of Judah, perhaps the most important of the 12 Israelite tribes.

LEVI—*American English pronunciation: LEE-vie. Hebrew pronunciation: lay-VEE.* The name may mean "joined" or "attached" or "twisted." Four different people in Scripture went by that name. The Levi mentioned in this book was the third son that Jacob and Leah had. He was the progenitor of the tribe

of Levi, from which the Jewish priests came. The Bible does not tell us a lot about him. He had three sons: Gershon (or Gershom), Kohath, and Merari.

NAPHTALI—*American English pronunciation: NAF-tah-lee. Hebrew pronunciation: naf-tah-LEE.* This proper name probably comes from the verb meaning "to wrestle." He was the sixth son of Jacob and the second son of Jacob's concubine Bilhah. Dan was his full brother. The Bible tells us almost nothing about Naphtali.

wife falsely accused Joseph of attempted rape. The father of Joseph's wife, Asenath, was also named Poti-phera. He was a priest in the city of On (later called Heliopolis), the center of sun worship.

RACHEL—*American English pronunciation: RAY-chel. Hebrew pronunciation: rah-HAIL.* Rachel means "ewe." She was Laban's daughter and the girl whom Jacob especially loved. Through Jacob's mother's side, Rachel was his first cousin. On his father's side, Rachel was his second cousin once removed. In order to win her hand in marriage, Jacob worked for Laban for seven years. (Jacob arrived penniless and so had no money for a bride price; additionally, Laban never gave either daughter the usual dowry a father paid.) To Jacob the time sped by because he had fallen madly in love with Rachel. Laban tricked Jacob on the wedding day, giving him Leah, Rachel's older sister, instead of Rachel herself, for whom Jacob had to work another seven years, though he got to marry Rachel at the end of that week. At first Rachel could not conceive, but finally she gave birth to Joseph and later Benjamin, dying during the latter's birth. When Jacob and his extended family left Haran and Laban, Rachel stole her father's teraphim or gods.

REBEKAH—*American English pronunciation: re-BECK-ah. Hebrew pronunciation: riv-KAH.* The name may mean "cow." Rebekah, daughter of Bethuel, lived in Paddan-aram until Eliezer, Abraham's servant, found her and took her back to Canaan to be Isaac's wife. She was Isaac's cousin once removed. Rebekah was barren for 20 years before she gave birth to Jacob and Esau. She favored Jacob, whereas Isaac favored Esau. She was buried in the Cave of Machpelah.

REUBEN—*American English pronunciation: ROO-ben. Hebrew pronunciation: re-oo-VAIN.* This male name probably means "behold a son." He was the first boy born to Jacob and Leah. When his brothers wanted to kill Joseph, Reuben worked to spare Joseph's life. Reuben had four sons

Reuben

(Hanoch, Pallu, Hezron, and Carmi). During the exodus from Egypt, Dathan and Abiram—both Reubenites—rebelled against Moses. Reuben's descendants, the Reubenites, were one of the tribes of Israel.

SHECHEM—*American English pronunciation: SHECK-em. Hebrew pronunciation: shee-KEM.* Shechem, which means "shoulder" or "back," was a walled Canaanite city in central Palestine. It was situated about 40 miles north of Jerusalem. Shechem covered nearly six acres of land. Abraham traveled here, and it was the first place where he camped in the Promised Land. Later Joseph, Abraham's great grandson, was buried here. Shechem was located near mounts Ebal and Gerizim. The city itself is at an altitude of 1,870 feet above sea level. During the time of the judges, a temple to Baal-berith (Baal of the covenant) was situated in Shechem. During part of its early history, a temple fortress was constructed inside Shechem. This new building had walls 17 feet thick! This temple existed for many years and appears to be the one mentioned in Judges 9 as the temple of Baal-berith. At the outset of the divided kingdom, Shechem served at first as Israel's capital city, which later was moved to nearby Samaria. In 750 B.C., during the time of the prophet Hosea, Shechem housed a shrine where Yahweh was worshiped. In 722 B.C. the Assyrians razed Shechem, but in 350 B.C. it was rebuilt, but John Hyrcanus destroyed it permanently in 107 B.C.

SIMEON—*American English pronunciation: SIM-ee-on. Hebrew pronunciation: shim-OHN.* Two biblical men went by the name of Simeon, which means "hearkening (to prayer)" or "answering (prayer)" or possibly "hyena"—one in the Old Testament and one in the New Testament. The Old Testament Simeon, the one mentioned in this book, was Jacob and Leah's second son. He was the progenitor of the tribe of Simeon. Simeon himself had six sons. When Joseph wanted to be sure that his brothers would bring Benjamin to Egypt, he imprisoned

Simeon

Zaphenath-Paneah

Simeon until their next visit for food. The territory in the Promised Land of the tribe of Simeon was in the southernmost part of Judah.

ZAPHENATH-PANEAH— *American English pronunciation: ZAF-nath-pa-NEE-ah. Hebrew pronunciation of the Egyptian word: tsah-fe-nath-pa-NAY-akh.* This was the Egyptian name pharaoh gave to Joseph when he made Joseph second only to himself. Records have not revealed other instances of this name until much later. The name

may mean "the god speaks and he lives." Such speculation behind this explanation of the name comes from the attested Egyptian proper name Djed-pa-netjer-iw-f-ankh. The Septuagint, the Greek rendition of the Old Testament, rendered the name Psonthomphanech.

ZEBULUN— *American English pronunciation: ZEB-you-lun. Hebrew pronunciation: ze-voo-LOON.* The name probably means "exalted" or "habitation." He was the sixth son born to

Jacob and Leah. He was the full brother of Issachar. Zebulun had three sons (Sered, Elon, and Jahleel). His descendants formed one of the 12 tribes of Israel, and their territory was in the highlands of Galilee. He was buried at the city of Aijalon.

ZILPAH— *American English pronunciation: ZIL-pah. Hebrew pronunciation: zil-PAH.* The name probably means "(woman with) a short nose." She was Laban's maidservant whom he gave to Leah when she married Jacob. When Leah, who already had given birth to four boys, wanted even more children, she gave Zilpah to Jacob as a concubine or secondary wife. Zilpah then gave birth to Gad and Asher.

RUTH REDDING BRAND

FINKLE PHOTOGRAPHY

Ruth Redding Brand, assistant professor of English at Atlantic Union College in Massachusetts, has written the main stories in this book. Bible stories have fascinated her from the time she was a child. When the Review and Herald Publishing Association invited her to explore the Holy Land with the late Siegfried Horn, a world-renowned archaeologist and imminently knowledgeable tour guide, she eagerly accepted. That experience (along with a lot of research) gave her access to an authenticity of detail that makes the narratives in the Family Bible Story books live and breathe.

Brand was raised on a dairy farm in Maine and grew up milking cows, haying, riding hefty workhorses, and pulling weeds in acres of corn and cucumbers. As an adult she has taught elementary school and junior high as well as college. Since earning her Master's degree in English, she has taught English at Fitchburg State College and Atlantic Union College.

She lives in Lancaster, Massachusetts, with her husband, Bob, and pampered cat, Sky. She is blessed with two adult children, Jeffrey and Heidi, and their respective spouses, Krista (Motschiedler) and Troy Clark. Brand loves to read, play word games, walk on the beach, and swim, but she'll drop any of these activities in a heartbeat to spend time with her granddaughter, little Miss Emma Mae Clark!

LINDA PORTER CARLYLE

Linda Porter Carlyle, who wrote the Bible bedtime stories for this book, says, "I love the poetry and the music of words. I especially take pleasure in writing read-aloud stories for the very young."

Carlyle lives with her husband, two beautiful daughters, one dog, three cats, and two rabbits on a quiet dead-end, tree-lined street. She homeschools her children, Sarah and Abby.

Among her favorite things are paper and pencils and pens. She also savors the quietness of a library, the smell of books, the feel of their pages, and the way the words look printed there.

Linda Porter Carlyle hopes that parents and children will be able to cuddle close to each other and enjoy—again and again—these Bible bedtime stories together. These stories also provide good exercises for beginning readers.

LEONA GLIDDEN RUNNING

Even as a little girl, Leona Glidden Running found foreign languages fascinating. In high school she learned Spanish from an older student who taught her during lunchtime. In college she majored in French and minored in German, which she later taught at the high school level.

For four years Running worked for the Voice of Prophecy, a well-known religious radiobroadcast originating from California, where she typed scripts in Spanish and Portuguese. During that time her husband, Leif (Bud) Running, died. She felt as though she were in a tunnel for eight years. Then she fell seriously ill, and when she recovered Running attended seminary, where she learned biblical Greek and Hebrew. From there she began teaching college classes in biblical languages while she worked on a doctorate in Semitic languages at Johns Hopkins University.

For many years Running taught ancient languages at Andrews University in Michigan. Even after her retirement she taught Egyptian hieroglyphics, Assyrian/Babylonian cuneiform, and ancient Syriac for 21 more years. Today Running enjoys total retirement from the classroom. She encourages young people with these words: "Find your gift, develop it, and let God use it!"

Leona Glidden Running reviewed for accuracy the stories in the Family Bible Story series. She also prepared the pronunciation guide at the end of this book.

CONSTANCE CLARK GANE

Born in Brunswick, Maine, Connie moved with her parents (Richard and Virginia Clark) to the mission field when she was only 6 years old. She lived for nine years in Nepal, followed by two years in Pune, India.

Gane attended Pacific Union College, where in 1986 she received her bachelor's degree in music with an emphasis in violin. For the next two years she and her husband, Roy, lived in Israel, where they studied at the Hebrew University in Jerusalem.

Her University of California, at Berkeley M.A. and Ph.D. degrees are in Mesopotamian archaeology. Gane has participated in archaeological excavations at Tel Dor and Tel Dan in Israel, the ancient site of Nineveh in Iraq, and Tal Jalul in Jordan. Her area of general interest is that of the ancient Near East under the dominance of the Neo-Assyrian, Neo-Babylonian, and Achaemenid empires. Specifically she specializes in *Mischwesen*, composite creatures, found in Late Neo-Babylonian religious art.

Gane currently is assistant professor of archaeology and Old Testament at the Seventh-day Adventist Theological Seminary at Andrews University in Berrien Springs, Michigan. She and her husband are the parents of one daughter, Sarah Elizabeth. Sarah keeps her parents in touch with reality and constantly turns their eyes and hearts to Jesus Christ.

JACK PENNINGTON

Jack Pennington, the artist who prepared the main illustrations for this book on Joseph, graduated from the Center for Creative Studies (now College for Creative Studies) in Detroit, Michigan. At the time of publication he lived in Washington Township, Michigan, with his wife, Marcia, and daughter, Kendall.

Pennington is an award-winning freelance illustrator who is especially in demand for his advertising artwork. He has illustrated for many well-known corporations, including NASCAR, McDonald's, Colgate-Palmolive, Coca-Cola, Harley-Davidson, BMW, General Motors, Toyota, Chrysler, Ford, and Kellogg's.

His hobbies include playing liturgical guitar and building and painting custom show cars. Some of his show cars, including a 1969 AMX and a 1966 Rambler American convertible have appeared in various automotive publications.

Pennington and his family have two dogs—Sparkle, a Shetland sheepdog, and Rambler, a long-haired mini-dachshund. They also have a pet fish, a hamster named Snickers, and a deer named Sherry. (The deer lives in the fenced-in area behind their house.)

Pennington's art studio and musical instrument depository are located in the third bedroom of their typical suburban ranch-style house.

DARREL TANK

One of Darrel Tank's earliest memories of art is drawing pictures with his mother. She encouraged his creativity, which was apparent even when he was a very small child. While growing up, he often spent his afternoons at the publishing house where his father was the head photographer. The work of the illustrators there particularly fascinated him, and he began to dream of pursuing a career in art.

Tank was able to accomplish that dream in the late seventies and has exhibited and received honors at numerous art shows with his sensitive approach to portraiture. His photo-realistic style shows remarkable attention to fine detail and captures the emotion of the moment.

Tank and his wife, Denise, have four children and 12 grandchildren. They live in Garden Valley, Idaho, up in the mountains where they have snow for three to four months of the year. He writes, "We are sur-rounded by meadows, forests of pines and firs, and groves of aspens. There's a tremendous amount of wildlife, including herds of elk and deer, foxes, bears, mountain lions, wild turkeys, bald eagles, raccoons, Canada geese, and so much more."

The Tanks have an "extremely smart" yellow Labrador retriever named Chamois. She knows many tricks and loves to perform them for visitors. They also have two cats. One is 13 years old and is named Sienna, because of her color. The other is a pure white, long-haired cat.

Tank's repertoire includes black-and-white pencil renderings, color pencil, gouache, airbrush paintings, and computer illustrations, which have appeared in more than 400 books, magazines, advertising, and prints.

ACKNOWLEDGMENTS

Where does one begin? So many individuals have helped in the construction of this unique book. We owe all a great debt of gratitude for the time and effort they invested to make the book a reality. Perhaps we can talk in categories of influence.

RESEARCH

Gail Hunt, who had the first vision of a multilayer book and then conducted 11 focus groups around the United States

Richard W. Coffen, who brainstormed with Mr. Hunt and became director of the project

Gerald Wheeler, who as a Bible lover and book editor embraced the concept

Patricia Fritz, who spent many hours coordinating myriads of details

Bob Haddock and Associates, who helped with early marketing plans

The **many men and women and boys and girls** who shared their valuable ideas at the focus groups

ADMINISTRATION

Harold F. Otis, Jr., president who caught the vision immediately

Robert S. Smith, president who insisted on moving ahead after years of delay

Hepsiba S. Singh, treasurer who offered the financial support needed

Mark B. Thomas, vice president of the Book Division, who helped facilitate development and chaired our oversight committee

Jeannette Johnson, acquisitions editor, who kept minutes for the Oversight Committtee

Trent Truman, art coordinator, who prepared the layout and design and worked with the talented illustrators who provided such amazing artwork

WRITERS

Ruth Redding Brand, who researched and wrote the main stories in this series

Linda Porter Carlyle, who wrote the Bible bedtime stories

Constance Clark Gane, who prepared the timeline

Leona Glidden Running, who prepared the pronunciation guide in the glossary/Bible dictionary

Richard W. Coffen, who wrote the DID YOU KNOW? sections

ILLUSTRATIVE ENDEAVORS

Jack Pennington   Darrel Tank

YOUNG READERS

Benjamin Baker	Nathan Blake	Annalise Harvey	Katrina Pepper	Bradley Thomas
David Baker	Coramina Cogan	Alyssa Harvey	Lisa Sayler	Jeremy Tooley
Emily Barr	Raeven Cogan	Garrick Herr	Emily Shockey	Tara Van Hyning
Jacob Barr	Rande Colburn	Alicia O'Connor	Katie Shockey	Kim Wasenmiller
Carin Bartlett	Zoë Rose Fritz	Jeremy Pepper	Jonathan Singh	Tompaul Wheeler
Caitlyn Bartlett	Jennifer Hanson	Jessica Pepper	Kaitlyn Singh	Megan Williams

SCHOLARLY INPUT

Douglas Clark	*Siegfried Horn*	*Pedrito Maynard-Reid*	*Warren Trenchard*
Larry Herr	*John R. Jones*	*Leona Glidden Running*	*S. Douglas Waterhouse*
Lawrence T. Geraty	*Sakae Kubo*	*Ronald Springett*	*Randall Younker*

LITERARY INPUT

Denise Herr, college English teacher

Kelly Bird, college student of Ms. Herr

Orval Driskel, marketer

Tracy Fry, college student of Ms. Herr

Susan Harvey, marketer

Eugene Lincoln, editor

Donna Martens, college student of Ms. Herr

Shelley Pocha, college student of Ms. Herr

Sherry Rusk, college student of Ms. Herr

Sandy Robinson, marketer

Sheri Rusk, college student of Ms. Herr

Doug Sayles, marketer

Gerald Wheeler, editor

Penny Wheeler, editor

Ray Woolsey, editor

EDITORIAL HELP

Eugene Lincoln, who helped edit and copyedit early versions

James Cavil, copy editor

Jocelyn Fay, copy editor

MISCELLANEOUS HELP

Ashraf Z. El-Khodary